The only
HR BEST PRACTICE
You'll ever need

LEADERS OFTEN MISS THE OBVIOUS IN PEOPLE MANAGEMENT

Wendy Giuffre
Ashley Kieboom

Publisher: Wendy Giuffre
wendyelleninc.ca

Library and Archives Canada Cataloguing in Publication
Wendy Giuffre
The Only HR Best Practice You'll Ever Need
ISBN 978-1-9991894-0-2 (pbk)
ISBN 978-1-9991894-1-9 (ebook)

Printed in Canada
Design by BluBrown Communications
Editing by Amphora Communications

Disclaimer: The material in this publication is of the nature of general comment only, and does not represent professional advice. It is not intended to provide specific guidance for particular circumstances and it should not be relied on as the basis for any decisions to take action or not take action on any matters which it covers. Readers should obtain professional advice where appropriate, before making any such decision. Although the authors and publishers have made every effort to ensure that the information in the book was correct at press time, the authors and publishers do not assume and hereby disclaim any liability to any third part for any loss, damage or disruption caused by errors and omissions, whether such errors or omissions result from negligence, accident or any other cause. The stories in the book, all names, characters, and incidents portrayed in this production are fictitious. No identification with actual persons (living or deceased), places, buildings, and products is intended or should be inferred.

It's about the people.

Organizations that are truly great, have leaders who have a deep understanding of that concept. Intuitively, they believe connection with their people and helping them to achieve success first is what ultimately leads to an exceptional organization.

We wrote this book to help leaders and aspiring leaders grow. We were able to do so because of the amazing people we've already had the opportunity to work with and learn from.

Thank you.

TABLE OF CONTENTS

FOREWORD

This is what some of our clients have to say about working with Wendy Ellen Inc.

Wendy and Ashley are in a class of their own when it comes to working with people through transitions. Success in our profession is often dictated by how quickly one can get people onboard and moving forward with a new strategy and direction. This process can take years if not handled correctly. We recently worked with Wendy and Ashley on a complex transaction involving ~120 employees across 8 locations in Canada. Their employee-centric approach was critical in helping us quickly move past 'transition' and into the 'performance improvement' phase of our investment.

– Tom, Private Equity Partner (US)

———————— ◎ ————————

I met Wendy Giuffre of Wendy Ellen Inc. a few years ago and quickly saw the value of her skill sets and what they could bring to our organization. The relationship we enjoy with Wendy has evolved to the point where she has become a virtual part of our team. Wendy is a dynamic resource whose skills cross many aspects of the Human Resources function that relate to our business.

She has been instrumental in helping us develop strategies, policies and procedures that support our dealership's goals. Wendy has shown significant value to our organization by introducing fresh, innovative concepts that are not industry specific which allows us to differentiate ourselves from other automotive organizations. Her value extends to supporting the leadership team to resolve day to day operational issues as required. Wendy has proven to be fair, credible and balanced with her counsel to employees and management alike. As a result, she has gained substantial credibility and respect throughout our organization. Wendy has alleviated the requirement to add a dedicated Human Resources manager as our organization grows.

– Andrew, Partner and General Manager, Auto Dealership

———————— ◎ ————————

With the ever changing complexities of Human Resources, changing regulatory environments and the dynamics of Gen Z to the Baby Boomers it is critical to have a trusted "HR" partner.

To navigate us through everything from developing policies, onboarding, retention and in-depth analysis of acquisition target's HR environment, Wendy & her team have provided us with timely and professional advice that fits with our culture.

– Randy, Partner, Acquisition and Management Corporation

CHAPTER 1

HR Best Practice? We don't have one.

*"To handle yourself, use your head;
to handle others, use your heart."*

ELEANOR ROOSEVELT

Anyone who has started a business or taken a leadership role in a company or other type of organization knows exactly how challenging it can be to ensure all the moving parts are heading in the right direction. One of the comments we often hear in the HR world is how much easier life would be if one particular 'part' was easier to manage — the people.

It's not that these leaders or business owners don't appreciate or value or have respect for their people. What happens is management tries putting policies and structure in place for working with them. If they don't work, they try others. This may be successful for awhile and for some of their staff, but not for all. Many of these business owners, leaders or managers arrive on our doorstep seeking the answer to these questions — "What can I do to keep my business/organization/department successful while also doing what's right for the people who work there? There must be clear policies or a guide on employee management that actually works? What are the HR best practices you can offer that will help things to run smoothly in our workplace?" As leaders or managers, they're frustrated because what they're doing isn't working and it's keeping them from achieving the success they are after and in many cases, is affecting the bottom line.

So, what is the solution? The idea of writing a book about what works for our clients after 40+ years of combined experience in the HR field had been percolating for a while. It had been about a month since our last discussion about it when we received a message from a client letting us know that his business had just failed. It was sad news because it had, not that long ago, been a thriving and successful enterprise for many years but had undergone a change in leadership about five years previously. Many people were now going to be out of jobs — at a time when prospects were dismal. What was even more unfortunate for these people was that this didn't have to happen. We were also not surprised by the phone call.

The company's previous owner had been a long-term client of Wendy Ellen Inc's. Before ownership changed hands, the company had no debt, owned the building it operated in and was busy all the time. Under the new ownership, the human resources philosophy was at odds with the former leader's. We continued to try to work with them, but the two new partners in the business were reluctant to keep wages and benefits on par with the rest of the industry, and there was frequent conflict between them, their people and even their customers and suppliers. We, along with the people who worked there, had no success discussing these concerns with them. Retention quickly began to dip and recruitment became a problem as this was a small industry. Word got around about the working conditions there and applications soon dried up. Our advice was rarely taken and over time, the amount of consulting we provided was minimal. It had been about a year since we were last engaged by them when one of the partners called with the news that they were out of business. He was asking for advice on resume writing for himself.

And with that distressing bit of news, we decided it was time to write this book. We wanted to share the wisdom gained from consulting with small to medium-sized enterprises and their people, and from a combined four decades of practicing in the human resources field. Our clients come from almost every sector including energy, technology, non-profit, engineering, insurance, retail, renewable energy, construction, hospitality, plumbing and mechanical, among others.

The question we are asked most often is "What are the rules or best practices in this situation with my employee or employees?" And so that's what we want to address in this book: the 'secret' or key to successfully 'managing people' that leaders, company owners and HR departments continuously seek.

Other than being compliant with legislation, we don't consistently follow any 'rules' or 'best practices'. We threw out the rule book a long time ago. Why? Because after many attempts to generalize an HR 'best practice', we realized there was no one-size-fits-all solution for every business or organization or for the people who work there.

If you are seeking a set of best practices or rules to follow to manage your people, you won't find it here — because we have never discovered it or came across one that works. All organizations and the people within them come with different cultures and personalities. A blanket approach just doesn't work. In this book, you'll notice we refer to employees as people. The reason behind this is because the word 'employees' takes away their individuality And that is what each and every organization, leader, business owner or HR team member is dealing with — individual human beings. Using the term 'employees' makes it easier to forget that it's people who are on the other side of the conversation, across the desk or reading the latest company-wide policy email. And in today's working world, the reality is there are so many different types of working relationships, the word 'employees' only addresses the traditional.

─────────────── ◎ ───────────────

When Wendy founded Wendy Ellen Inc. in 2005, she made the choice to work with small to medium-sized enterprises. Early on, she began to see that applying the same best practices and policies she had to employ while working for a big organization to all of her clients and their people didn't work. Every client had its own unique characteristics or culture, and the people who worked for them didn't arrive at the office having shed their individuality. In 2012, she invited Ashley to join her as a consultant (Ashley had decided to leave the large energy company she worked for — her strengths as an individual weren't recognized and there was little opportunity for growth).

———————————— ◎ ————————————

Both of us started our careers in the human resources departments at large oil and gas companies who applied strict best practices policies; we've experienced them and we've attempted to apply them. At massive companies it may be necessary to employ policies that are used across the board and apply to everyone. However, each of these immense businesses are also made up of many departments or teams, which are similar to a small or mid-sized business in which people can and should be treated as individuals.

Over time, it became more and more apparent to both of us that the rule book didn't work for our clients. People rarely react in the way you expect.

With that in mind, we created a fresh approach to the people-side of our clients' organizations. Our shared vision was to use more of a grassroots process for the organizations who engaged us and those that worked for them. We both had previous experience working at policy-driven, bureaucracy-heavy organizations and with the people who dealt with that type of an environment on a daily basis. And we didn't enjoy working in those workplaces nor did we think it was successful in smaller enterprises.

It certainly wasn't working well for our clients. Both of us believed HR didn't need to be highly structured. We also understood fighting that battle in many larger organizations would be challenging, if not impossible — wide-scale policy should exist in larger corporations, for many reasons. What drew us to this world is what is often also appealing to the people who choose to work for them — the flexibility and the opportunity. Many of the people we have worked with while consulting with our clients say they didn't want to be part of the rigid structure of most big companies. They all felt as if they were put into boxes in these organizations and that it was difficult to stand out and grow in those situations (Ashley had her own personal experience of this).

We decided we wanted to work with our clients to create environments where leaders and business owners didn't struggle as much to deal with employee relations issues — where they were able to provide the kind of leadership and a workplace where people loved to come to work every day, where everyone could shine and where they could achieve their own goals within the small to medium-sized business world.

We also realized early on, both for our clients and for ourselves in the human resources field, that working with people means the need for difficult conversations about many issues: performance, compensation, absenteeism, among others. We've had our share of awkward ones such as co-workers complaining about loud eating or a lack of deodorant. Believe us when we say nothing surprises us; we've had to address it all in one way or another.

What happens with many of these issues is the rule or policy book gets pulled out. Or there are several phone calls, emails or meetings to decide how to deal with the problem. How are we going to handle this? What's our strategy? What's the worst case scenario? This is similar to an avoidance tactic because everyone dreads having the conversation that needs to take place.

Our experience has been that it's difficult to predict how the conversation will go. People typically react poorly to being called out on their behaviour if it's done with condescension or reprimands. Being honest and direct, having empathy and trying to understand the situation from the viewpoint of the person sitting across from you, almost always leads to a more positive outcome. When faced with honesty and a frank face-to-face conversation, most of us will be more open to the discussion and to finding solutions.

We recently were hired by a company who was having dress code issues with some of their people. At the time of hiring, everyone who was employed there read and signed on for the same policy (which was actually an extremely liberal dress code). We were hired because a few people continued to fight the dress code and wear inappropriate clothes to the office. Otherwise, the company had no problems with them — each of them had great performance reviews. They had tried sending out a reminder to everyone, which had no effect. So we were brought in to address the issue one-on-one with the people causing the problems. We sat down with each of them on an individual basis and talked about their specific way of dressing. What came out of each of those conversations was drastically different. One person was worried about money and had financial constraints — she couldn't afford to buy new clothing. We made some suggestions which helped her to be part of the solution. Another one really didn't understand the inappropriateness of his clothing and quickly adjusted. The third person was furious and continued to dress inappropriately. These three situations needed to be handled differently and no 'best practice' could have told a manager how to deal with the problem. A second frank, face-to-face conversation had to happen with the third person and if the problem continued, decisions would need to be made to manage the issue on a more permanent basis.

That is just one small example of the many workplace issues faced by employers. There are a range of challenges businesses face during the HR life cycle — from recruiting all the way to terminations, and everything in between — and many different ways to solve them. In writing this book, we talk about what has worked for us and our clients. At the core of everything we do as consultants is a practice of using empathy, honesty and ingenuity. Other than being compliant with legislation, that's our only philosophy and we believe it's the only one leaders, business owners, managers and HR teams need.

To demonstrate the types of workplace culture and people management issues which occur during the HR life cycle and our solutions for them, we have created fictional companies and fictional people who work for them. All of these stories are based on a compilation of experiences and clients we have worked with over the years and do not represent any of our clients or their organizations, or anyone who has worked for them. We begin in Chapter Two with Leadership, where company culture originates; from there it trickles down through the organization. In each succeeding chapter, we take you through the points in the HR cycle where potential problems can, and likely will occur, and our approach to solving them. Our goal was to create scenarios that are typical of HR concerns and how they often play out in the workplace, and through the characters and stories we developed, demonstrate what our advice would have been and how we would have solved those types of people issues. Throughout this book, you will come across situations that will crop up during the various stages of the human resources cycle of your organization. And we have no doubt they will appear! We hope this book will help you to create a more successful workplace for both you and the people who work with and for you.

———————————— ◎ ————————————

HAPPY READING!

Wendy & Ashley

———————————— ◎ ————————————

CHAPTER 2

Because I'm the boss

─────── ◎ ───────

We all get frustrated. Whether you're a leader or on the frontline, our philosophy is that everyone, regardless of job title, needs to be treated as a 'human being'. Whether that person ranks below you in the 'company hierarchy' or is someone you report to, treat them with respect, courtesy and understanding.

─────── ◎ ───────

It's been our experience most people don't show up at work having shed their personal lives at the office door. People typically arrive at work as the same individuals they are at home or elsewhere. And sometimes they come with pre-conceived beliefs about their roles.

People show up at the office with all their flaws, foibles, quirks and bad habits. Most of them are likely dealing with issues in their personal lives, whether it's family, relationships, health or financial concerns. The degree to which their personal lives are being affected by those concerns is going to impact their work lives. And in turn, your business. There are few of us who can successfully compartmentalize what's going on at home from our roles at work. We are all just trying to do our best, and on days when we might be struggling, are going to fall short of what's expected by the people we report to at work. With all of that to contend with, how as a boss, manager, leader, VP or in-house human resources professional, do you succeed?

What we find works best for the leaders and managers we advise is to always remember this one important thing — this is a person sitting across from you. And yes, they are also an individual who works for your organization and who has responsibilities. But they are much more than just that, more than an asset or number or role. There is no question it's frustrating as a leader or team manager who has goals to meet and their own people to report to — higher-ups, shareholders, business partners and so on — when one of your people is experiencing some challenges and not fulfilling the role they were hired for as expected.

It can be easy if you're in a management or leadership role to get caught up in focusing only on productivity or meeting objectives. For-profit companies are in the business of making money. If that becomes the only priority as a leader or manager, and you interact with your people without considering they are the very key to achieving your productivity goals, it's likely you are going to run into significant people relations issues.

A successful HR strategy always has your people as an integral part of your business strategy. And all of these people come with their own diverse set of skills, strengths and accompanying human weaknesses, or as we like to call them in the Wendy Ellen Inc. world, 'improvables'.

If the leadership team doesn't take this into consideration, you're going to hit a wall of resistance at some point. It may be that personal issues are affecting a person's ability to work, or they may need to be able to work differently. This is someone who is being challenged on some level. As one human being dealing with another, always remember that one critical point — your people should be a priority.

Our advice? If that person is struggling with 'performance' in the office, the questions to ask are: Why? What's going on? How can I help?

There's a second, really important thing we recommend to our clients. Create simplicity in company policies and processes. While businesses need to have some policies and expectations in place, they still need to remain flexible and leave room for the 'grey areas'.

> *"Life is really simple,*
> *but we insist on making it complicated."*
> CONFUCIUS

Conversation, talking things through, rather than pulling out a binder to see 'how we deal with that here' resolves issues much more satisfactorily and quickly than a three-day string of emails and meetings to adhere to bureaucracy.

We've all heard the saying 'people leave their jobs because of bad or difficult bosses'. It's true. When a person or team member is treated with disrespect or without considering what may be happening with them to impact their ability to perform, there will be ramifications. Whether it's through less productivity, poor performance, frequent absenteeism or in some cases, disruptive behaviour in the workplace or worst-case scenario, resignation, the results of this type of leadership or management will be felt and seen.

Our focus is always, no matter what your role or level of seniority, to treat others with respect and to get to the root of a problem through discussion, rather than relying on policy to find solutions.

Paradoxically, since we're all human, that doesn't always happen! In some cases, past work experience has shown some of us it's acceptable to show disrespect at work because "I'm the boss".

> *"It's always been a mystery to me how people can respect themselves when they humiliate others."*
> MAHATMA GHANDI

A few years ago, we were approached to solve a human resource issue in a web design company. Glacier Interactive Marketing was a successful web design company with about 100 people — the average age of everyone, including most of the leadership was mid-30s, or a bit younger. One of the department managers was a woman we'll call Paula. The team led by Paula was struggling — performance was down, people were unhappy and the level of absenteeism was increasing.

Paula was 32, single and had come to Glacier after several years of working in a large energy company where she had been part of the IT department. A self-described 'computer geek', she had started out as part of Glacier's back-end development team. Highly skilled, she worked long hours and it was clear she had gained significant knowledge and experience in her previous role. She could be quite funny, often regaling her co-workers with stories of her latest adventures in the dating world, and everyone on her team enjoyed working with her. Logan, Glacier Interactive's President, was impressed enough by what he observed and by her manager's reports to give Paula her own team to manage. That's when things began to go awry. After her promotion, whenever she was in a meeting with her team, or working with any of them one-on-one, she became dictatorial and demanding. The Paula they had known and liked became all business. When she was frustrated because goals weren't being met, often spoke to members of her department in a condescending way, handing out directives and walking around the office monitoring who was in their offices and hard at work.

We were brought in by Logan to work with Paula and to get the team gelling again. It was our first time consulting with Glacier and Logan appeared to be a great leader. In his 40s, he was a bit older than everyone who worked for him. He was easy to talk to and charismatic; as a serial entrepreneur, he was confident in leading the company. Glacier was growing quickly, which was one of the reasons he had promoted Paula — their clientele was expanding. Although there were now serious issues with Paula, everyone enjoyed working with Logan, and loved their jobs.

What came out of our one-on-one meetings with Paula and in separate meetings with Logan, was that this behaviour by Paula wasn't who she was as a person outside of her role as department manager. In our individual meetings with her, she showed up as someone who was friendly and personable. In the meetings we had with her and Logan, her behaviour changed again. Although she and Logan appeared to have a friendly relationship, she often deferred to him in our conversations. It was a striking contrast to the person she appeared to be. Although driven and hard-working, she had a great sense of humour and when she wasn't interacting in her role as a manager with her team members, we saw someone who was approachable, warm and genuinely friendly.

She had an image of what a boss should be. In Paula's mind, bosses are … bossy. When she was in her role as department manager, that's the persona she slipped into, and when she was with Logan, the company

President, she changed her behaviour again. We called it her 'boss hat', which she would slip on and off when she thought it was needed.

As we continued to work with her, we learned that from her perspective a manager had to be tough. In her role as the head of the team, she couldn't show vulnerability; she needed to speak in an authoritarian voice and avoid any chit chat. There were goals to be met, and when they weren't being achieved, she would act on her frustration. Paula was acting the way she thought she needed to from ideas based on old school role modelling. She may have seen these types of office scenarios take place in her past role, or from observing a parent who might have been in a managerial role, or it could have been advice she received from that parent, a past colleague or a friend. It was a bit of a Jekyll and Hyde situation, as if she had two personalities. Or perhaps three? Who she really was, who she thought she had to be in a managerial position and the person who reported to the President.

In our work with Glacier, we also saw that it was a bit of an 'old boys' club'. The company was led by Logan and most of the people employed there were men. As Paula was one of the few women working there, she may have subconsciously felt she couldn't show any softness or vulnerability.

Whatever the reasons were, her methods weren't working for the company, the people she led or her. Her team members were complaining about how they were being treated and some were ready to leave the company, although they were reluctant to do so because it was, for the most part, a great place to work. There were many opportunities and everyone loved working with Logan.

When we initially met Logan, we saw someone we would consider the true definition of a 'leader'. Logan positioned himself as one of the team, although everyone he worked with understood he was still the President and the decision-maker. He was well respected and well liked; he listened to ideas and he wasn't afraid to say, "I don't know". Because he was very entrepreneurial, there wasn't a lot of structure or bureaucracy. We thought this helped to create the loyalty the team had towards Logan. Paula brought a great deal of expertise and knowledge to the company; this may have been why he was willing to go to such lengths to help her with her 'improvables'.

Our role was to help Paula build the skills to improve her leadership abilities and break down the paradigm she had created. After meeting with her and having some conversations, we could see she had leadership skills. She just didn't know how to deploy them — we needed to be the facilitator. We worked with her in a coaching capacity to help her be herself and allow her natural leadership skills to come through in her various roles.

Damage control was required which was impossible to do overnight. Again, we dealt with the damage caused by her behaviour through conversations with her team, who were made aware senior management was working with her to enhance her skills and ways to improve her relationships.

In our ongoing work with Paula, we focused on discussions about specific situations. We had many conversations with her about skill sets and offered different tactics on how to 'lead' instead of 'boss'. Paula was given a lot of coaching on softer skills and options on how to interact with her team in different situations. Being their leader was not as easy as being their 'boss'.

We gave her some simple and common sense ideas. Most of our advice as consultants we view as 'common sense'. First thing in the morning, say "hello"; not to check if your people are in, but simply to say "hi". Have conversations with the people who report to you, don't talk at them or just fire out directives. Ask them how they're doing; what they did on the weekend; how are the kids doing?

Working with Paula sent a positive message throughout the company. Instead of terminating her, Logan was willing to work with her to solve these serious concerns and to offer her the opportunity and support to improve her ability to carry out her role. Her team members respected company management for recognizing there was a problem and for working with Paula on it. Because of her expertise, she had moved up in the company quickly and, as they had known her before her transition to the 'boss role', they may have felt some loyalty towards her because of shared history. They were all committed to the company and knew Paula was valuable because of the knowledge she had brought with her. As people hired by the company, they also had some comfort around the fact the President and management chose to work with Paula to fix the issue instead of terminating her. If they later moved up in the company, and ran into issues, that was good information.

Rather than acting as many businesses would have — adhering to 'company policy' — and letting Paula go, Logan chose to act in a more humane manner and help her. This may have caused some short-term discomfort when we were brought in to consult and resolve the behavioural concerns. In the big picture, by making this choice, the company benefitted in several ways. There was no need to replace a department manager (a significant cost and disruption); company culture was strengthened because the people working there could see the President of the company valued a team member enough to try to resolve the problem; and Paula's loyalty to the company soared because of the opportunity she was given.

It's critical to have transparency within the company's human resources area. Always leave the door open for further conversation. People need and want to be heard even though there are times when you can't, or choose not to, fix the problem. Everyone goes into a job or role with certain expectations — sometimes those are misaligned with company values or culture. There may be assumed expectations from the people-side when they come onboard. Leaders need to be transparent and clear about those expectations. Paula had assumed expectations around her role and possibly, company culture. Perhaps a conversation about 'how we do things around here', wasn't addressed fully with her when she came onboard.

This story about Glacier Interactive, Logan and Paula underscores a deeply held core value at Wendy Ellen Inc. and how we work with our clients. People are people. They are going to make mistakes. Instead of looking at them as easily replaced roles or just as an employee, work with them in the way they would like to be treated. Get to know your people and understand where they are coming from. Figure out what their skills are and how you can best develop them. How you handle issues or respond to problems is likely not how they would react in the same situation. Understand that and work with them at their level, not yours.

Don't treat them as disposable, like a commodity to be thrown aside when it's no longer useful. In the long run, your organization will build more loyalty which usually translates to happier customers, reduced turnover and a place people want to come to work every day. All of this leads to a healthier bottom line. If there's one thing we've seen that has contributed the most to the building of a strong, sustainable business, it is the creation of a work environment where people love to come to work. Happy and engaged people means repeat customers who will choose to do business with you, instead of your competition.

In some cases, leaders will take the opposite approach to those who view their people as expendable. We have worked with some clients who take the phrase 'go the extra mile' too far. There is a fine line between wanting to make your organization feel like a family and treating your people as such. Going above and beyond, they make workplace accommodation past what is necessary. Some will go as far as to help the person financially (without the proper paperwork in place) or continue to employ some people far longer than they reasonably should have, given the circumstances. For many reasons they may not want to let the person go; they may really like the individual and have known them for a long time. Their circumstances may be quite difficult as the result of a termination. We don't recommend keeping someone on that should be terminated — it's difficult for the people they work with, who may have to pick up the slack or deal with a difficult personality. There are several solutions for managing this type of workplace situation and we talk about that further in Chapter 10.

About five years ago, we worked with a client with a small leadership team of four partners, which employed about 95 people. When we were brought in, the company was struggling to meet its business goals and the work environment had become seriously dysfunctional. The company had been in business for about three years. It had some early success because the founders had captured a market niche that no one else had at that point. Now, it had run into problems — the bottom line was heading in the wrong direction, objectives weren't being met and most of the people were not functioning well in their roles.

After conversations with the leaders and with some of the people, we uncovered the issue. It wasn't the product, it wasn't the business model and it wasn't the people (although they had definitely contributed to the problem). From day one, the four business owners had chosen 'to be the best employers' they could be as one of their core values. Their hearts were in the right place, but the problem was the execution. They were literally bending over backwards 'to treat people as people' to the point of being detrimental to the functioning of the business. Decisions about compensation and scheduling were dictated by individual people's needs and the leadership spent so much time addressing the wants and needs of each person, it was difficult to focus on the business. While we advocate strongly for accommodation, this can be taken too far in a direction which will adversely affect the company and other people who are respectful and don't expect to be catered to by their employers. It's pretty simple — most people want to be heard, and expect reasonable accommodation. If they are also committed to the company, they will know when a request is unreasonable and they won't make it. If a pattern persists of always making exceptions/accommodations, even these reasonable individuals may start to expect the same treatment and you will have a people management problem.

Some people may have many medical appointments or, if they are part of the sandwich generation, appointments for children or an elderly parent. As long as they are getting their work done on time and the rest of the team isn't affected, our approach is to ask these questions: Are your needs being met as an employer? What is your priority here? And if your needs are being met, why are we having this conversation?

What happens when you don't treat people well? When you don't look at them as individuals? You get less commitment, more absenteeism and higher turnover. When the economy is good, people will leave and they'll also spread the word you are a poor employer. In today's online world, that's easy to do. There are websites created specifically for this purpose — an online space where current and former employees can anonymously review companies and their management. If you treat your people poorly, you will not present well on these sites.

With social media, your reputation is only as good as the way you treat your clients and the people who work for you. The proven best way to recruit is through referrals, which you won't receive if you have a culture of disregarding individuals. If someone has left to improve their skills, think about boomerang recruiting. If they have had a positive, fulfilling experience at your organization, they may return in the future and bring their newly acquired skills with them.

If one of your people is doing a poor job and you've looked at options to help them, and the situation doesn't improve, our advice is to end their employment. If they are just taking advantage and getting whatever they can, terminate them. If someone is struggling, find out why. People have 16 hours of life outside of work and as much as they may try, it can be challenging to leave that at home.

And yes, you must always consider this from the business perspective. As we talked about earlier, there are ways to help someone without it affecting the company's bottom line. With that in mind, you still need to keep business decisions as business decisions. There are so many resources out there and many opportunities or ways to make changes without affecting your business. As a business leader, it's critical to have boundaries — this is where some employers have difficulties.

From another perspective, we counsel our clients that time spent on the job is not always the most important measurement. Instead, are the deliverables being met? Why would you not accommodate someone for a shorter commute time at 7 instead of 7:45 as long as it works for your business? Does it matter what time they arrive if the job is getting done? This is the box that employers often try to use but doesn't always work. We have clients who need help to see outside that rigid structure — not everything fits within rules and regulations. The world has changed;

people expect to have a life outside of the company. Keep it simple and reduce the bureaucracy.

If as an employer, you only provide the very basics, you're going to see that behaviour reflected in your people. Even if your business is all about the product — the question still remains: who builds the product and who sells it? It's still people. It's not a long-term approach to have a bad culture. If many of your people are unhappy and retention is low, what's the human resources strategy you are using? Specifically, what's the reason you are acting as if they were disposable? What's the business case for having a disregard for people and their workplace satisfaction? Employees, just like customers, have choices and options. They will leave and go to work for your competition.

It should feel good as an employer to treat your people well — it's the right thing to do. And it's common sense. Why wouldn't you treat someone the way you'd like to be treated? Even better, the way they would prefer to be treated and, if you can help them be more successful in work or life, do it. Not all companies and jobs can accommodate doing this, but if you can, why wouldn't you?

CHAPTER 3

Look up — that's where it all begins

Great Leadership Traits

It takes work to be an incredible leader; to consistently walk, talk and behave with leadership qualities.

Leadership is something you have to practice — being faced with challenging situations and resolving them with empathy, logic and tact, while keeping the business in mind, is a skill you will need to continue to hone throughout your career.

Before we begin to go through the first step of the HR cycle, recruitment, it's critical to talk about what we believe is the most important aspect of organizational success (in addition to the people who work there) — leadership! The best companies almost always have a great leader at the helm. Someone people want to help succeed. Someone people want to emulate. Someone people believe understands who they are and how to help them succeed. And yes, there are 'successful' companies with poor leadership where the employee experience is dismal. In our eyes, success means a profitable company with a fulfilling people experience — which usually means great leadership. Companies that lack that type of leadership may achieve success at any cost, but we believe it won't be long-lasting and eventually the truth will come out.

It's impossible to hide bad behaviour in today's world for any length of time. At the companies where this type of behaviour is condoned, if you ask the people employed there, they will tell you they are treated poorly. Low wages, impossible work quotas, 12-14 hour work days, and more are the 'normal' expectations as these companies rake in the profits. There is no shortage of these tales. If this is the truth about those workplace conditions, that type of culture is typically fostered from the top, trickling its way through the entire company.

At a truly great company, where profit and market share are not the only drivers, where there's a humane approach to achieving goals, where an environment of collaboration and empathy is nurtured, someone with true leadership qualities will be heading the organization.

If you're applying for a senior role, you're going to interview with other senior people. Make sure you also interview them and talk to other executive positions at the company. Be aware though — people are often reluctant to give you the goods, the whole story; watch body language as it will tell you a great deal. It's a big red flag if someone gets twitchy and appears to be avoiding your questions. This works both ways — for the interviewer and the interviewee. Your intuition is a powerful tool; listen to your gut. Nine times out of ten it's right and you may need to explore further or decide not to pursue the opportunity.

———————————————— ◎ ————————————————

So, what makes a great leader? Along with an infallible code of ethics, a great leader needs to be empathetic, genuine, transparent, and smart; common sense is another essential quality. We put empathy at the beginning of the list because we believe it's the most critical attribute.

As a CEO, you may have many balls in the air and have the ability to manage the pressure easily. If someone who reports to you doesn't have that same capacity, our advice is not to expect that person to be identical to you in the way they respond to responsibilities and workplace pressure. Remember, everyone that works for you, no matter in what capacity, comes with their own set of styles, strengths and 'not so strengths'. They may have a different work style and method for getting results. When we work with CEOs, leaders or managers, our recommendation is always to match your expectations to the person (assuming, of course, you hired someone with the right skills for the job).

———————————————— ◎ ————————————————

The people you are leading are not mini-me's.

———————————————— ◎ ————————————————

Where we observe the most success (including financial) is in workplace cultures where the leader is someone who understands this concept and coaches people to work to their strengths. It all boils down to being empathetic. An exceptional leader has the ability to understand the other person's perspective, which may be very different from yours. This type of leader will allow, and often encourage, dissimilar styles.

A truly great leader will dig deep to understand who they are leading and look at them with a view to seeing more than just their roles or responsibilities. This type of leader will consider who they are as the whole person. They will understand their people's strengths and weaknesses; what makes them tick and what creates enjoyment and success for them. A truly great leader will modify their approach with each person to help that individual not only to accomplish what's expected of them but to be even better in their role. A truly great leader will take the time to find out what 'success' means personally for each team member and support them in getting there. And in doing so will create a team with long-term loyalty.

For that to work, we believe it's impossible to successfully lead a large team. You can manage a large team but leading an effective and extensive team is different. Someone who comprehends this will be smart enough to build a team of people who will foster this culture of empathy within the company to their individual direct reports. This sets the foundation for this type of culture to trickle down to create a workplace where this code, this way of treating other team members and people, is paramount. In contrast to organizations where a culture of fear percolates throughout, in this workplace, a culture of authenticity, empathy, support and camaraderie will develop and thrive.

Making a conscious decision to be that type of leader won't necessarily get you there. Many leadership traits are innate; typically someone who excels at leadership was a natural leader from the time they were in grade school. It's challenging, if not impossible, to go from being a follower to being a successful leader — our personalities don't function that way. Just making that decision alone in most cases doesn't work well unless the basic traits are inherent. For someone who has leadership qualities, but is a 'diamond in the rough', those skills can be honed through experience, coaching and mentoring, moving them from good to exceptional.

Although we believe leaders need to have those qualities of empathy, honesty and authenticity, their individual approaches will be different. By definition, someone who leads typically 'goes their own way' and doesn't follow the pack. They have a vision and they want to see it come to fruition. A steadfast confidence in themselves and their ideas exists, and from that follows a strong belief in their people.

A true leader will be able to:

- Delegate and give opportunities to others

- Recognize talent

- Listen and learn

- Engage with the team and others

- Adopt a hands-on approach

- Make decisions

- Admit to and move on from mistakes

We can't all be leaders or there would be chaos! If there are people who lead, there must also be those who are led. These individuals don't want to be the decision-makers or bear that much responsibility. They are more fulfilled by helping leaders carry out their visions. Being in charge has no appeal for them — they have different aspirations. Just like a leader is driven towards a future goal, success for that individual has a different meaning. And there is nothing wrong with that. There are times when these people are categorized as unambitious or even lazy. When we talked earlier about empathy, someone with great leadership skills won't make that assumption (although there are most definitely people who are unmotivated and that's another issue) and will find out what motivates this person. This type of leader will work with them to make it possible to be successful in their role, working to their strengths and bringing the best out of this person.

Where we often see problems begin in leadership or management positions is when someone, who is highly skilled and has worked at the company for a lengthy amount of time, is promoted. They are then thrust into a supervisory or managerial position. It appears to them and those around them, that this is the only way for them to progress through the company. There is no question about their ability. Some don't even want to assume this responsibility — they are pushed or promoted into it. This usually becomes a failing situation for the person, the company and for the people who report to them. An exceptional leader who has taken the time to understand their people will know who is destined for leadership and also, perhaps more importantly, who is not a candidate for a leading role. We don't believe those individuals who don't have leadership qualities can be 'rehabilitated' and turned into leaders. There are inherent leadership skills which can be learned — communication skills for one, but the built-in combination of a take-charge attitude and empathy (among others) won't be obvious if a person isn't a natural leader. A leader with well-developed communication abilities and who is empathetic will have the ability to deliver bad news without crushing someone, while a poor one will focus on the negative and accentuate what went wrong, usually leaving a person feeling dejected and unmotivated.

For those who have ended up in leadership roles purely through promotion and haven't been successful, a role needs to be found where their expertise is needed and appreciated. Have an honest conversation with them — most of the time they are already aware it's not working. Talk about other opportunities to grow. It's important to be creative in how you work with these individuals who are valuable to your company and bring many other skills and experience. They can lead projects, not people, and be responsible for deliverables, but not carry any managerial responsibilities. Trying to push a square peg into a round hole is not going to create success for your company or your high-performing individual.

Our advice has been to recommend creating a different role or a niche for those people, so they still rise in the organization but as a specialist or a subject matter expert. By doing this, their skills are recognized and utilized, the company benefits and people remain happy and engaged.

We worked with one individual whose expertise was in software engineering. He was brilliant at his role, but having people report to him was disastrous. He was good at teaching but failed miserably as a leader. We recommended he become a specialist in his area, a guru whom other team members could access for knowledge. This worked exceptionally well — he was happy and the company had someone in place who anyone could refer to for technical questions or assistance. It also fed into his ego in a good way, allowing him to feel important, needed, respected and productive.

─────────────── ◎ ───────────────

At one time, Wendy worked at a company where it was the next level of management that came together in understanding the weakness of the organization's leader. She and her colleagues worked around the leader and learned not to rely on him. As a team they were able to make their strategies work and the company was highly successful; on an individual basis, it would have been challenging to work around this leader. The team really believed in the company, and understood what they needed to deliver to him to make things progress. Working together they made it doable. It isn't common for this to be successful, but in this case, it was because of the team.

———————————— ◎ ————————————

Companies will, on occasion, try to remedy a problem where leadership is lacking by throwing money at the situation, especially when times are flush and revenue is up. Giving someone who is unhappy a raise is a quick, easy and usually unsuccessful Band-Aid fix to a problem. Our experience has been most people aren't in it only for the pay cheque and will eventually leave. And when there's an economic downturn, throwing money at a problem is not always easy to do.

At one point, we worked with a client who symbolized the best of leadership qualities, someone to this day we try to emulate and coach others to do the same. In a meeting we attended, he faced nine managers sitting across the table from him, arms crossed and tempers simmering. By the end of the day, their attitudes were completely changed. Why? It was his style. He was calm, transparent and organized; he never let them rattle him and he came across as honest and authentic (which he was). He didn't overpromise and was forthright about what he knew and didn't know. What also won him points was the fact he spoke little and he listened a great deal. Not once did he use the word 'but'.

I learned a lot from this client. There were times I was part of conference calls with 20 people or more (all integral to the project at hand) and he managed the meeting like we were all sitting around a table. He recognized everyone by voice. Everyone had a fair chance to speak and he managed emotions so well it was as if he could read their body language. He was present and focused. It was just who he was.

—Wendy

One of the companies we worked with for a long time, until it was acquired, was Big Sky Architecture and Design, which had about 90 people on staff in three different offices. Travis, who was the COO, was one of the best leaders we have ever had the opportunity to work alongside. He had a great deal of business savvy and we never heard anyone say a bad word about him. In his mid-50's, Travis was married with two teenagers and was clearly focused on growing the business and himself. He knew when to be the boss — when to draw the line. In the location he operated, Travis acted like a part of the team (ate lunch with them every day, always the first to say yes to getting a coffee, knew details about everyone's kids and pets and weekends). Everyone still regarded him as a leader. It was almost intangible, but everyone just knew. People wanted to please him and do good work for him; no one wanted to disappoint Travis. He had tough conversations when he needed to have them and made decisions quickly.

He led by example — he worked hard, kept meetings running smoothly and didn't leave things to the last minute, expecting someone who reported to him to get the more tedious details done.

Although Travis was not a micro-manager, he always knew what was going on in the office with his people and handled things quickly if there were issues. He understood his weaknesses and what he didn't have time for, and was wise enough to realize when he needed to outsource some of the work, which is how Wendy Ellen Inc. became his HR presence.

I always enjoyed working with Travis. I miss working with him and Big Sky since the company was eventually sold.

–Ashley

One of the other partners who managed a separate location, Allison, also married, was the President. She was definitely intelligent and had a keen sense for the business; our perspective was that she was more average in terms of her people management skills. We didn't see the same type of leadership abilities as Travis, and her focus seemed to be more on making a profit (not understanding that through good people, the profit would be made). During the time we consulted with them, we didn't get to know her that well, which in and of itself makes a statement. We heard many complaints about Allison from her people. Her style was more of a top down type of leadership and few of her people felt engaged with her, and we saw a definite lack of motivation in her team.

Matt, the third partner, was in his early 40s and single. He was the Vice President of Innovation and ran the third location. His team all viewed him as more of a friend than a leader. Matt wasn't taken seriously and because he travelled so much, was rarely in the office. When he was there, he didn't have the time to devote himself to being a good team leader, although he was equally as intelligent as Travis and Allison, and highly skilled at his position. He truly wanted to be a good leader but it always came last. The main complaints we received about Matt were the lack of time he had to help his team grow and progress in their roles.

The different styles of leadership were beginning to take a toll on the company's bottom line and its retention. Travis initially brought us in to consult on this and to help them find a solution.

Matt definitely had the best intentions and possibly the skills but too much on his plate. Our questions for him were directed at finding out if he really wanted to be leading people, or if he would be better suited to focusing only on the technical side? We also saw times where some people behaved too casually with him; they saw him as too much of a friend and that didn't help his leadership presence. As a leader, you have to understand where that line is between friendship and leadership, and stick to the boundaries.

Allison was not what we considered a great leader. As one of the founders of the company, she was brilliant as an architect, so felt she 'had' to maintain leadership responsibilities. She didn't know her team at all on a personal level. Allison stayed behind closed doors in her office most of each day, but felt she was creating relationships and 'mingling' with people when she walked by and said "hello". She was not at all transparent or approachable — her team generally didn't know what she was involved in on a daily basis or what was going on with the company. We believed she had an 'old school vision of corner office president' and behaved that way even in this small company. Because of that, she may have felt even more pressure to act like a 'traditional president' to legitimize her role. In the process of modifying roles, the company was acquired so the end to this story is that they went their separate ways — which often happens in a large company.

What we saw underscored our belief about leadership — Travis, the born leader, excelled and his team was cohesive and happy in their roles. Allison and Matt, who struggled with leadership positions, had fewer natural skills and never thrived as leaders or with their teams.

Over my career, I have worked with three incredible leaders who were mentors. All of them had an impact on the trajectory of my success.

−Wendy

If you find yourself in a role not suited to your personality or your abilities, seek advice or mentorship. Look at the options available — if you love what you do and believe in the company/product/service, do you have the right people reporting to you to be successful, to still create an environment where your people are engaged? If not, is there a workaround? Can you still lead but build a team to support you? Can you hire someone to lead alongside you? Even the best leaders need support. The best advice we can give is to always play to your strengths and utilize other resources to fill in the gaps.

While poor leaders can still attract good people initially, they don't often keep them. The mask can only stay on for so long and flaws will eventually reveal themselves.

People leave bosses, not jobs. They seek mentorship and opportunities to improve their skills throughout their careers. If you're not receiving that, why waste your time? From a 'people' perspective, our advice is pretty straight forward when you find yourself working somewhere with a poor leader. Leave. That may sound harsh and too simplistic, but in most cases, it is truly the best decision. Obviously, it depends on what you are looking for, but if it's exposure to new challenges and mentorship, which we believe are the most important aspects in career progression, you're doing yourself a disservice if you remain working at the company. If you find yourself in an organization with failed leadership and you decide to leave, take the time to do some research and make a conscious choice about the type of organization you choose to work in. Life is short. Too short to be stuck in a role you're unhappy in, where the people surrounding you are just as miserable, or to be working for someone who creates that kind of misery. Perhaps even more importantly, we don't recommend staying at a place where you are not nurtured and are not growing.

———————————— ◎ ————————————

Great leaders attract great people. Others want to surround them, to be part of their circle, to help them fulfill their vision for the future.

An exceptional leader understands it's about the people. At a deeper level, they believe it's the connection with their people, and helping them to achieve success first, that ultimately leads to an exceptional organization.

CHAPTER 4

Be slow to hire and quick to fire

"Hiring the right people takes time, the right
questions, and a healthy dose of curiosity."

RICHARD BRANSON

One of the specific areas where we often see companies run into problems within their HR processes is in the first step — recruitment. The biggest issue? Management and/or the HR department take far too long to hold the interview or to have follow-up interviews. The process gets stalled for one reason or another; the organization's people who need to be in the interview or follow-up interviews postpone or reschedule, often more than once. What happens then is that they lose the engagement of the good candidates and typically have to start the process over again. This sends a poor message to the person who may still be in the running. The best candidates will also be hired elsewhere before the process is finally complete. We believe it's critical to start off by creating the proverbial 'good first impression' and show that you value this person, their time and the role you're trying to fill. You may have the opportunity to interview the candidates that are still available after a long recruitment process — but it will likely be those who are less in demand. If they have given up in frustration and begun interviewing elsewhere, your company is then in the position of starting over with a search for new candidates, which can be a costly and time-wasting situation.

The first step when beginning the interviewing and hiring process is a commitment to the exercise, whether you conduct it with an internal team or hire an HR consultant. The second step is to have a clear understanding of the role for which you are hiring — but we also recommend being flexible. One of the clients we worked with didn't have a firm grasp on what she was looking for in a candidate. We brought her the right people with the appropriate qualifications, but she couldn't make a decision. What eventually transpired for her was positive — she needed to take a step back and figure out which role/task/accountabilities she was searching for. We worked with her to develop a better strategy. We looked at the gaps in her organization: Where did she lack expertise? What skills was she missing from a tactical standpoint? What leadership strengths could be well utilized within her organization? Together, we looked at all aspects of the new role she was trying to fill. Then we began the search again, and funnily enough, some of the original candidates fit the role perfectly. This round of interviews was far more successful because she had a clear idea of the skills she needed in her organization.

Another example, where an organization we consulted with wasn't clear on what they needed in a role before they started the search, took a different, but yet again, successful turn. The leader knew he wanted to expand his business. The search for this person wasn't to going to be easy due to the specific qualifications he sought. Candidates were brought in for interviews with varying backgrounds, all with slightly different strengths. After interviewing a few qualified and interesting people, this business leader realized that he could expand his business in a different direction than first thought by hiring one of the candidates who presented with slightly different skills than we had been seeking. This individual brought a perspective so different from the business owner's that it opened up a new avenue for business growth. There are times when you think you know exactly what you want, and have the all the details in mind, and a surprise candidate shows up that may be as, or more, effective. When filling a very defined role, such as a basic accounting position, this isn't likely to occur. You know exactly what is needed for the accounting role. Roles that have more general responsibilities and room to grow leave more opportunities for different types of candidates. In this case, where the client had a more general accountability for this new role (expanding the business), keeping an open mind was a blessing.

Having all the qualifications also doesn't necessarily mean the person is right for the role. Personality can be just as important as technical skills, especially when a company is in growth mode. Naturally, there are skills you are looking for, but attitude, character and a good fit are equally as important. When seeking someone for a client-facing role in customer service or administration, they need to have the right personality. Many of those job skills can be taught and in many cases, the best decision would be to choose a candidate with less skills if they are a better fit.

The dreaded resume selection process is an opportune time to improve your selection methods. This process has its challenges both when we have a strong economy and the job market is tight, and also when our economy is suffering and the market is overflowing with candidates. When times are good, it can be difficult to find the right people. In a strong marketplace, the exercise is more than just resume mining — you often have to actively search for the best candidates, typically with the help of search consultants. When the economy is weak, it can also be challenging as there are hundreds of resumes to dig through and it can be an extremely time consuming and frustrating experience. Again, it's often why many companies turn to search consultants. In the case of a slower economy where your company is inundated with resumes, you may not need a search consultant, but rather an extra body (preferably with HR experience) to help you weed out the unqualified applicants, of which there are usually many.

Some HR teams and consultants discard any resumes containing a typo. We don't necessarily agree with that practice — you can be excluding some great people. If that person makes it through to the interview stage, it is worth a mention that they should have had someone proof their resume, but you thought their skills outweighed the 'one typo' issue. If there are many typos, discard it. Obviously this is someone who pays no attention to detail, doesn't care or is applying to so many roles, the role being offered is not important to them. One thing we do look for is creativity. Resumes that stand out for one reason or another illustrate that the individual has put time and effort into creating it — the same thing you would want them to put into the job. It also shows that they understand the need to stand out and will make the effort to do so. Creativity in any role should be welcomed as that is how growth and improvement can occur.

We often ask in an interview, "Other than the skills on your resume and the experiences we have discussed, what else can you as an individual bring to our organization?" This goes back to the premise of this book — people are individuals. What will they bring as a person, not as a role, to enhance your company? How will they make your business a better place to work? As an interviewer, these other skills can be worth considering in the role and as an overall benefit to the company. If you think someone may be a good fit for the company, find out how else they could be an asset to your organization.

As an interviewer, if there's a gap in the resume, we recommend asking why. It's not necessarily a problem; sometimes it can be a positive.

Perhaps they took a year to travel — that can add to a person's skillset in many other ways — or they were caring for an aging parent?

Personality, Personality, Personality

Of all the boxes we look to check off when hiring, we believe personality, along with a sense of humour, are the top characteristics for which a company should recruit. For many roles, some skills aren't as critical as being a team player who's fun and enjoyable to work with.

When someone isn't nervous in an interview, that should set off the alarms. It could mean they have been on so many, they no longer feel any stress about the interview. Occasionally, this is also a sign of indifference — definitely not a trait you would want in someone working for your business. Someone who is somewhat anxious, and can manage the nervousness, is a positive sign. Manageable stress can bring out the best in people. The adrenaline associated with that stress often allows them to be on top of their game. It also shows how they would perform under pressure in the job. If an individual is so nervous that it impedes the interview process, that should be a red flag for the same reason. This could be a sign as to how that individual will perform under pressure, which is unfortunate for the candidate, but it's critical for your organization. And again, personality and showing a sense of humour is another good omen.

There are strong advocates of pre-determined interview questions and protocol. We also see the advantage of free-flow interviews, so we recommend a hybrid. Obviously, there needs to be a standard set of questions as part of the process, but you also need to explore the answers. If that aspect is skipped, it will be difficult to get a good understanding of who this person is and what makes them tick. At Wendy Ellen Inc., we look for people who have stories to back-up their skills. It's within the free-flow part of the interview where you will hear these stories. We want to hear how they solved that problem, how they reacted in that difficult situation. Stories also give you an insight into personality; keep the person you are interviewing talking and continue to probe. This takes them away from any pre-fabricated answers and will give you much more insight into who they are. Allow an answer to prompt another question. During the interview you obviously have to find out whether the individual has the skills for the job, however, following a hybrid between free-flow and pre-determined questions allows for 'personality' to come through. Ensure everyone in the room also has an opportunity to ask questions and to shake it up a little. The pre-determined questions are more important for some roles than others, particularly highly technical roles, where a straight comparison between candidates is important. This is also why it is important to have more than one person interviewing — technical people often interview in a structured manner, where people managers or HR professionals tend to have a more free-flowing personable interview. The combination can create a near-perfect interview.

Going for coffee or lunch when you're getting closer to the offer stage is another good practice. It allows you to observe your potential team member in a more relaxed situation. It's a great opportunity to find out more about them; at lunch or coffee, conversations may come up that will give you answers to questions you can't technically ask in a formal interview. We heard about one company we thought had an interesting strategy: the recruiter invites the candidate and team members at the offer stage out for lunch to a restaurant — it's always the same restaurant and its staff have been cued ahead of time to have someone 'mess up' the order for the candidate to see how they handle it. The company believes the candidate's treatment of the restaurant staff when they've made a mistake is a good indicator of that person's character and personality. It's not a bad idea!

In an interview situation, if there is something that bothers you or doesn't make sense, pay attention to your intuition. It can be a gap the interviewee is reluctant to explain. Or if they hesitate when you ask if you can call references — this is one area where red flags often pop up. It can often be they didn't get along with their supervisor, but the key is to find out why and make your decision based on that. Always listen to your gut. Always pay attention to red flags.

Typically it's easy to tell when someone is making something up. It's why we prefer casual interviews — there's a lot more opportunity to ask additional questions and to probe. If they aren't forthcoming, try to find out more.

As with any situation in life, there's likely a reason for the hesitation. Read between the lines. Trust your instincts. If you still think that person would be a good fit for your company, proceed to the next step. Perhaps that is offering them the job. However, if they have all the skills, but you still feel something is off, cut the interview process short.

Be slow to hire — or you may find yourself in a position of having to terminate someone in the future. When we say 'slow', we mean taking the appropriate time to get to know people. This does not mean putting off interviews or making the process needlessly lengthy; this is where you will lose candidates. Taking your time before bringing someone into your organization is wise. If they end up not being the right fit, the cost of training them and then having to re-train someone else is significant. There's the disruption to your business as well as the impact on the other people who work for you. If you have let the situation go past the legislated probationary period, you will need to factor in the cost of paying severance. When in doubt, go with your intuition and look for someone else.

We had an experience several years ago with our client, Glacier Interactive, the website design company we wrote about earlier, with someone who interviewed well and had all the prerequisites. We made the offer and he accepted; Logan, the President, hosted an annual barbecue and we invited the new team member. Both during the barbecue and into the next day, several of the female staff reported back that they were uncomfortable around him. It was nothing they could put their finger on, but they found him 'disturbing'. He had already quit his previous job, but we still rescinded the offer. He was highly qualified but we had to listen to our people and respect their intuition – and consider the potential for serious issues in the future. Logan and Paula placed a great deal of faith in our advice and went with it. Fortunately, for the company, and for him, the market was good at that time and he quickly found another position.

It's also essential to understand why someone is applying for the job and whether it's the right reason. It can't be just for the money or just because they don't like their existing or past role. They need to want to work for you and your company and grow their skills and progress in their careers. We also look for confidence but not arrogance. There is a huge gap between these two and for us it also means the difference between being the successful candidate and cutting the interview short. We seek people who are keen to work, to learn and to mentor, and who are not afraid to roll up their sleeves when needed, even in a senior role. If an interviewee indicates they wouldn't be willing to get their hands dirty, that's a red flag.

Making the right hiring decision is so important to the well-being of an organization. If it's a technical bad hire, an enormous amount of time is needed to retrain that person. If it's a wrong hire because of personality and attitude, it can destroy your culture. Take the time upfront to see the candidate from all angles and then make your decision — which, by the way, may still not be the right one.

This is why there is a legislated probationary period; it has been created for an important reason. That person may just not be a good fit — either technically (the skill set was misrepresented) or culturally. This is why it's so critical to do your due diligence pre-hiring in the many ways we've described in this chapter. Personalities can also do a 180 degree turn after someone has been hired. It's not that common but happens occasionally — someone thinks they are secure, they may shed the mask and their true personality comes through, one you had no idea existed. Because of this, we often get asked about extending the probationary period. In the eyes of employment standards, that does nothing. You will still have to give someone their due notice under the standards legislation, no matter what the individual agrees to. Extending probation really has no purpose; within three months, you should have a good idea of whether this is the right person. Most roles take six to nine months to develop a good grasp of what's required, but from an employer's standpoint, you should know within three months whether you've made the right decision as far as fit. If you still aren't sure after the three month probationary period, and you have some concerns, we suggest putting together a strong performance plan with clear expectations, strategies to get there and an end date for evaluation. It should be clear that if this plan is not successful, the relationship will likely end (even though you will still have to pay out the notice required).

Bringing some of your team along for the pre-hire lunch is also something we recommend strongly. Communicate this doesn't give them veto power, but they can provide feedback. In the situation like the barbecue we talked about earlier, that could have saved us from a potential bad hiring mistake. Ten years ago, we might have suggested trying harder to work with that person, and to give them a chance. But experience has taught us, if something doesn't feel right, if it's not working, it's not likely going to. Personalities won't likely change.

Advice for jobseekers

If you managed to get to the interview stage, and you know you don't necessarily have all the required skills, show how your other skills/traits can be an asset to the organization. Highlight these and how you can apply them to this organization along with what the benefit would be to the company. Play to your strengths — if you're someone who is a good mentor, talk about how much you enjoy that role and how this would benefit some of the other staff — are you able to craft a mentorship program? If you're a great writer, expand on that and how you can assist some of the other people. If you have specific interests, such as nutrition, bring that up and explain that you would love to hold a lunch 'n learn sometime. Show how you can add to the company and bring other positives to the role.

If you are someone who is submitting a resume, look for some connection to the company when writing your cover letter — "I saw this on your website and" …… or "I grew up five blocks away from your office and I passed it every day on my way to school. I always wondered what was going on inside your building." By adding some sort of personal connection to the company, it shows that you have done your research and that you are not just 'throwing' resumes out to every job ad. Cover letters that include something about the company, whether it's a personal connection or not, show the applicant has done their homework and knows what the company does. Adding colour or an innovative resume design also makes a resume pop out from the rest. Sometimes it's appropriate to ask questions in the covering letter — it can capture the interest of the person doing the recruiting. That being said, make sure it is thoughtfully done and not just throwing in colour or crazy fonts just to be different. It's never a good idea to include pictures.

───────────── ◎ ─────────────

From a management perspective, while the recruitment process can be tough, it can also be fun, provide great team-building and bonding over the search for the right fit for your team. Try to enjoy the process and laugh over the humorous things that almost always occur. We have seen everything, from candidates showing up drunk to awkward run-in's with ex-spouses; candidates wearing dirty sweatpants or breaking the computer in the office trying to show us a PowerPoint presentation.

—————————————— ◎ ——————————————

One time, while leaving an interview at a client's, a candidate hit my car on the way out (accidentally!). The poor guy almost died from embarrassment, he felt so awful. He didn't get the job (unrelatedly) but we're sure he thought that was why….

—Ashley

—————————————— ◎ ——————————————

Our best advice in the hiring process is to be 'slow to hire and quick to fire'. These are not our words but an old HR adage. You will save yourself and your company a great deal of time, money, wasted effort and be able to maintain the culture you strived so hard to create.

CHAPTER 5

First impressions — your mother was right!

"First impressions are the most lasting."
PROVERBS

The first two weeks of a new team member's experience at your company can be a deciding factor in how successful they are in their role. In fact, there are studies that show those first weeks, whether those initial days are a success or a failure, are tied to the longevity of that individual's time with your company. When it's a non-existent or unorganized onboarding experience, it's likely they may not stay for the long-term. First impressions do count. And it's so easy to provide a positive onboarding experience. There are many interesting and inexpensive ways to show a new person they are welcome and their presence is appreciated.

If someone is scrambling for the first few days, trying to figure out where things are, who they should be connecting with and feeling under-utilized, it's going to leave them with a bad taste. In this case, the people that you spent valuable time bringing into your organization may start looking for a way out sooner than later. They may assume the experience of their first few days with the company reflects on what their general experience will be like. As well as a poor first impression of your company, it's also an expensive mistake for the business. Productivity is lost as the new person takes longer than necessary to get up to speed on the new role. Your company has spent time and money to hire this individual, why not start day one off right?

We often see this happen with summer students. They're hired because the company wants to groom them for a future full-time position. Frequently left under-utilized and bored, especially at the beginning, they often aren't interested in a permanent role because of their experience. Instead, with a thorough and innovative onboarding program, they could be learning more about the company and be more productive if they are offered a full-time role after graduation.

A great onboarding experience means starting to prepare immediately after the offer has been accepted. The basic onboarding program itself should be well established, but preparation for the individual begins at offer acceptance. The manager or supervisor of the new person knows when they will be starting so they need to kickstart the program and allocate time to spend with them.

Once the offer letter is signed and before day one, send the new person an email with all the information needed to make the first few days a success. Explain what the first day will look like, who they should ask for when they arrive, anything they need to bring (i.e. void cheque, know their SIN) and if there is anything the company needs to know about them that would make their first day more comfortable. It's important to ensure they feel welcome. We all want to feel special and included. Let them know if you'll be taking them for lunch so they don't have to bring their own — or tell them you have a fridge available for whatever they bring. Attach all the necessary paperwork and benefits information in the email and ask that it be completed beforehand or that it be brought on the first day, along with any questions.

On that first day, there should be someone to greet the new person. Their office or cubicle should be ready with a clean desk. There's nothing worse than sitting down to a dirty desk and keyboard, with tatty stationery and someone's old coffee mug ringed with coffee stains — it's common sense but people are busy and it's one of the things that often gets overlooked. Ensure that there is stationery and business cards (if necessary) ready. Leave an organization and seating chart on the desk so they can familiarize themselves with who is who in the company. A company phone list is a must — these are usually online so ensure, as part of their IT tutorial, they are given instructions as to where all the company directory information is housed. We also think it's a nice welcoming touch to have some company swag waiting for them — a company coffee mug and a Starbucks card is a suggestion — along with a card with a welcome aboard message from the President or CEO. It doesn't have to be expensive, but it's these little details that can make all the difference.

We also highly recommend assigning the new person a 'buddy' or someone in the vicinity that they can rely on to help with the nuisance issues, office protocol and to direct them if they get lost. People want to know — Is it okay if I go for coffee? How does the scanner work? I don't remember the washroom code? Where do people go for lunch; do they eat at their desks or in the lunchroom? Trying to figure this out on your own as the new person can be frustrating and, for some personalities, unnerving.

All those suggestions are free and simple; they help to set the stage for the first few days to be a positive experience. Again, common sense. Put yourself in their shoes; what would you want to know/have? Remember what it was like for you on your first day. Whether this person is the new receptionist or a senior manager, everyone has the same needs and apprehensions.

More than just your employee

I've learned this myself with new people and running my own company. It's really crucial to do this. You don't get to know them as a person unless you make the effort. It's important to take them out for lunch that first week to find out who they are on an individual basis, what their interests are, ask about their family, hobbies and pets — the things you don't find out in the interview process. Doing this sets the foundation for a stronger relationship in the future and a much more engaged person. It shouldn't end the first week. Make an effort to go for coffee/lunch periodically (more so in the beginning) so you really get to know them. You should be doing this with all your new people throughout the first month and getting your team together so they can also learn about their new colleague.

–Wendy

Another simple way to ensure the incoming person feels welcome is to send out an email the day before advising other team members that someone new is starting tomorrow, where they will be sitting and what their role is — and ask them to introduce themselves and help make it a great first day.

Organize a lunch for the first day or week so they can get to know other people in the department or the team. It's also important to make sure there is work to do the first day, so they can feel like they are contributing.

Some companies have a PowerPoint presentation and safety orientation which helps with meeting other people in the company and getting to know the lay of the land. Ideally, all businesses should have a corporate video with leaders and real-life staff talking about the culture and sharing anecdotes about the company. These are great ways to provide information to new people and to help them get a feel for the company. Part of a great onboarding package is developing a series of activities or exercises where the new person must go out into the company to research things about colleagues or the company (if possible, for a real project) and make it interesting — almost scavenger hunt-like. Once they have completed the onboarding program, have them present to the company (if size permits) or the team on their findings. This allows them to practice their presentation skills in a safe place, along with a little humour hopefully, to break the ice.

At the location managed by Travis, the COO at Big Sky Architecture and Design (the company we introduced in Chapter 3), he had designed a full day of meet and greets for new people including a lunch and a job shadow. He also implemented the type of onboarding exercise described above — a week-long scavenger hunt where the new individual had to find out information about various team members (nothing embarrassing, please), roles, projects and leaders' nuances. At the end of that week, the new team member presented their findings over a team lunch. A small prize was given afterwards, usually in the form of company swag. This was effective in many ways — the new person learned much more about the company and new co-workers than they would have typically in the first week, and more importantly interacted with others in a non-threatening way. It was a brilliant and innovative way to help to learn about the company; we highly recommend other companies also consider this idea.

Travis also implemented another onboarding program that took place over a six-month period. Pre-scheduled lunches were held on a weekly basis with him and the team for the first month, and then with the department manager for a three-month follow-up. After that he scheduled sit down meeting check-ins and then brief touch-points at certain intervals, which would taper off over time.

Travis' attention to detail, when it came to the experience for the people who worked for him, was why his team was so successful. This was apparent in their contribution to the bottom line. Retention at the location he oversaw was significantly better than other locations.

As people get busy, it's easy to forget someone is still new — it typically takes about six to nine months for someone to settle into a position. Having scheduled meetings is ideal. They shouldn't be about performance management, but more to check-in to see if the expectations of the person are being met. It's a good way to ensure you ask questions about whether you're helping them to be successful and if the company is meeting their needs as an individual.

At Wendy Ellen Inc., we create onboarding checklists for our clients which are preferably paperless (there are some good software options for this). They provide new people with access ID and onboarding paperwork. If you don't have the capacity to purchase software, this can still be done with paper — always ensure there is follow up with the individual on the paperwork side and someone for them to call, such as the HR administrator or HR consultant (not the boss), so they can ask what they may consider the 'stupid' questions. The paper side of onboarding is a basic necessity; creative programs as we described with Big Sky earlier are where you get the long-term benefits.

If the onboarding experience has been poor, be transparent about it; acknowledge that mistakes were made. Being honest goes a long way. Explain that this isn't how your company wants to make its first impression and talk about how you dropped the ball. People are generally understanding if you're open and honest. And going back to the common sense approach we advocate — to be blunt, it's not rocket science — approach them as you would want to be approached if something similar happened. And then make a plan so the following week is better. Always ask for their input — how could you have made this a better experience for them? This is a good exercise to do periodically during feedback sessions with your people. Ask anyone with under 18 months or so with your organization how you could have made that time better, more comfortable, more successful? What did they need from you that they didn't get?

Mistakes happen. We've had situations with clients where the manager or team lead the new person was to report to ended up going on vacation or inadvertently took the day off. A simple apology and providing them with everything you can makes all the difference.

One of our clients was an insurance company which had hired a summer student who sat there for three or four weeks with nothing to do. We would go into the office and see her sitting there looking completely bored. We kept prompting the managers to assign her some work, but they were so busy in their day-to-day work that they didn't take the time to see how they could have offloaded some of that work, and accomplish two things: engage the student and lighten their own load. At first, it is more work to offload, explain and mentor students. In the long run, hopefully it will take some of the work off your desk and more importantly engage that individual so they will be interested in returning. Otherwise, why did you hire them in the first place? We did end up finding some meaningful work from several individuals in the organization and put together a project that no one else had time to do and which allowed the student to learn and use some of the skills she had acquired at university. She ended up accepting a full time position with the company.

Take the time when you're not busy to create a task list for new people. Enlist the input of the team. Be creative and don't just give them make-work projects. If you hired them in the first place, there must have been a reason and a role for them.

When we have a client with a new person coming onboard, we take the time, late in the day before they're starting, to clean their desk and the keyboard and ensure the office is set up for them. It should look like new and smell fresh — a little effort and Lysol goes a long way.

On our recommendation, Travis at Big Sky Architecture also implemented the onboarding procedure we talked about earlier when someone new was hired — a welcome card signed by him placed on a clean and clear desk stocked with enough stationery to get started; a freshly dusted/wiped chair; wiped down walls with non-essentials removed; business cards (if applicable); name plate; a company lanyard; and mug and a Starbucks card for the shop down the street. Whenever someone new started, a welcome email was sent out that morning and someone was assigned to take them around to meet everyone else upon arrival. This is something we recommend to all of our clients.

It's pretty simple to give someone an outstanding onboarding experience, but you need to be organized and prepared. Over the long run, it's going to save you and your company time, effort and cost. You've gone to the trouble of hiring this person — make sure the first day and first weeks are everything you would want them to be if you were in their shoes.

CHAPTER 6

I can't feel my toes

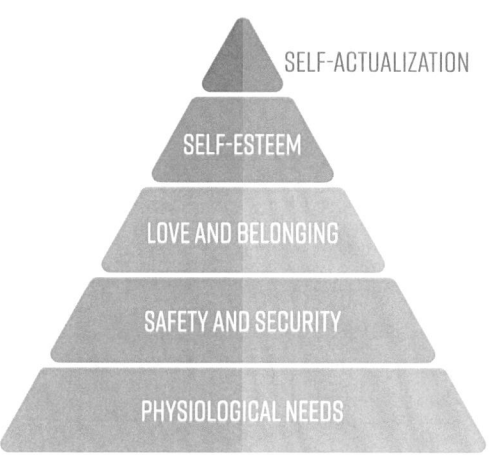

If we look at Maslow's Hierarchy of Needs above, the first tier of human needs is physiological. According to his theory, the first four needs arise because of deprivation — the longer the need is unmet, the stronger the motivation to fulfil the need becomes. So, if someone is physically uncomfortable, the longer they remain that way, the more they're going to be driven to find a way to ease their discomfort, before they begin to move up the pyramid to fulfill the other needs.

One of the most critical, but often overlooked, ways you can create engagement and retention is to provide pleasant and comfortable surroundings for people to work in. If your people are not physically comfortable where they spend 40 hours a week or more, it will be hard for them to enjoy their work.

If people are sitting on uncomfortable office chairs, enduring an office that is either too hot or too cold, slaving eight hours a day in a dim environment with little light or coping with other challenging scenarios, they're also not going to be as productive because their focus will be on relieving their discomfort. This is going to be a distraction; they are likely going to get up more often to move around and stretch, or go outside to cool off or, if your office is really cold, to heat up! People shouldn't have to adjust their clothing to manage the office temperature, or drink cup after cup of coffee in order to stay warm. And most of us are aware that lengthy periods of exposure to artificial light may be unhealthy both physically and emotionally.

At one of our previous clients, Stampede Manufacturing, Sarah, age 55, was the President and CEO. She had immigrated to Canada in her late 30s. She didn't understand Canadian employment legislation and hadn't assimilated to our culture. She didn't seem to have a strong belief in the role of HR; her behaviour was often dictatorial and demeaning.

People brought in deck chairs from home rather than try to work on the cheap and rock-hard office chairs available. Because the office was so cold— Sarah wouldn't spend any money on the heating system — most of them worked in parkas and gloves or sat there shivering because of the working conditions. Every Friday was a day off. They earned this day by working a longer day the other four weekdays; most of them didn't leave their office chairs for nine hours on those days. Meanwhile, Sarah was sitting in a spacious corner office with lots of natural light, dozing in her chair, next to a space heater.

She wasn't frugal across the board — one area where the company would spend money was on client functions. The bill for one of its functions was just shy of $100,000. It was obvious that it was an expensive affair — this was a slap in the face for those who worked in those conditions especially when only 60 percent of them attended the party.

The working conditions were so bad, Sarah and the rest of the management team would seldom bring clients to the office and planned to meet them elsewhere. On the rare occasions when it was unavoidable, people were warned ahead of time not to wear their outdoor gear.

Interestingly enough, although turnover was very high (no surprise there), some people developed a strange loyalty to the company. It was a small and highly innovative startup company with a unique product. They wanted to see it through, so they were willing to endure high levels of disrespect in how they were treated and tough working conditions. Their devotion was, however, misplaced as leadership was never able to move fast enough with the planned innovations and the competition sprinted ahead of them. It was somewhat along the lines of the little engine that could, and wanted to, but just never did.

It's easy to get laser-focused on creating revenue and achieving quarterly goals. To think only of the big picture. That mindset may serve you well in the short term, but it's in the details of how you get there that make all the difference for longevity. If we go back to Maslow's Hierarchy, where the first need is physiological, when that need for physical ease is unmet in the workplace, people respond with lower productivity, they respond with lower engagement and they respond with lower retention.

Again, it's just good practical sense. If we sit down to work at home, we first ensure everything is at hand to make ourselves comfortable. Lighting goes on or off, window blinds up or down, temperature higher or lower; we get the right cushion for our chair, clear off our desk, make ourselves a cup of coffee. We get set up to get things done. At home, our office space and the rest of our environment have also been personalized. Pictures hang on the wall, photos of our families, friends and pets surround us, a vase of flowers sits where it can be seen and enjoyed. We spend so much time in our homes — why wouldn't they be designed to be pleasant and enjoyable?

The same can be said for the office or workplace. View the working space you offer, or are creating, through your people's eyes. It's about the feel. Which would you prefer — a bland, uninviting and uncomfortable office or cubicle? Or one that is welcoming, warm and where it's physically easy to spend most of your waking hours?

The way you approach this conveys a strong message about how you value your people. Creating a work environment people want to spend time in and enjoy doesn't have to be an expensive endeavour. Competition is high in this area; decent and reasonably priced office furniture is available everywhere, online and in nearby brick and mortar locations. It doesn't have to be high end — more importantly, it needs to be functional and comfortable.

There are many options to create a workspace your people will enjoy without breaking the bank. One of the ways is to encourage them to personalize the area where they work, to make the space their own.

Many organizations today have remote staff and work stations where anyone attending the office can plug in. Those, of course, are difficult to personalize, but by choosing the right furniture and providing dividers for privacy, you can create a more aesthetically pleasing space.

One of our clients had purchased a company; we worked with them on the acquisition. At the company being bought, although they all received a good salary and amazing benefits and perks, the working conditions were, to say the least, challenging. The workspace was filled with old furniture and not enough of it; there were piles of boxes everywhere, little natural light and was poorly designed. Safety standards were nonexistent. To use the one and only printer, just about everyone had to walk quite a distance and then stand in line for sometimes as much as 20 minutes. Our client was not in a position to offer anywhere near the same level of salary and benefits. When we met with the people who were employed at the original company, she came prepared with a visual package of the company history, and showed them pictures of the local office space and social activities with the promise of securing similar space for their operation. She asked each of them in individual meetings what was important to them in their physical workspace. Was it important to have natural light? Would they prefer an office in a quieter area of the building? What kind of chair would they be most comfortable in? Everyone employed at the purchased company signed up to come and work for her at the new company. The working conditions were so much better, they outweighed the monetary differences.

It's similar to the difference between a well laid-out store and a disorganized, chaotic one that is smelly and dirty. In one, you'll want to spend time and in the other, you'll head for the exit as soon as possible. Environment can be mood changing. And it helps if it's designed to be conducive to team work and social chit chat. Whether it's open office space or walled offices, having inviting areas where people can come together for social conversation, work collaboration or just to step away from their formal space to do some work allows for increased productivity. Think about the times when you are working from home or a different space, how a change of scenery can allow for creative and productive juices to flow.

For those who spend most of their time working on a computer, their desks and chairs need to be set up to be ergonomically friendly and it may be difficult for them to concentrate in an open environment. If giving them individual office space isn't possible, incorporate dividers, plants, etc. to provide some separation. In an open environment, you need to have an office culture that allows for the noise and disruption factor — and where respect is shown to one another. Even with open areas, personalization to a certain degree is essential; a soft radio playing in the background, some art and photos on the walls, plants, etc. In an open space, to keep ambient noise out, allowing people to listen to music on their phones or other devices is completely acceptable in our books.

Even in an office that is primarily an open area, provide both a communal meeting place where people can collaborate and some private office space. Leadership and HR both need individual office space in any organization for the same reason. If a conversation needs to take place that, for any number of reasons should be kept confidential or one-on-one, having the participants unexpectedly move into a special meeting room that has been set aside for that purpose, can start the gossip mills churning or cause disruption for others. Human Resources definitely requires a private place and, although glass walls or doors can look pretty, they are open to whomever walks by.

Space should also be provided where personal calls can be made away from an open space or office, without fear of being seen or heard. We all need to make those calls during the workday at one time or another. Trying to call a doctor or phone a spouse/partner or child from a cubicle is awkward and no one should have to be put in that position. Open area offices need to be done well; they need to be conceptualized and designed thoughtfully.

Companies which have communal lunch space and cultures where their people are encouraged to take a break and engage with the rest of the team on a social level, have better productivity overall. Even better are the organizations with leaders who choose to join them.

I was working with a client who had a beautiful space including areas with plenty of collaborative and meeting spaces, all of which were either open or enclosed in clear glass. I remember this one time I had a young woman in one of the glass meeting rooms and she was crying. People were strolling by and could clearly see her. It was uncomfortable and unpleasant for everyone. Although the space was well designed, the glass enclosures didn't allow for privacy. If you were having a meeting in one of those spaces, people would stare as they walked by. It wasn't intentional or malicious, just a natural reaction. It's also human nature for them to talk about what they saw.

–Ashley

When the company's financial situation doesn't allow for much, or any spending, be open and transparent about it. Tell your people, "We don't have the money (right now), so bring us your ideas". In this situation, management needs to be flexible and allow their teams to be creative. It can include bringing a different chair from home, or volunteering to bring in plants, fish bowls, etc., (make sure they also agree to maintain them) and allowing people to express their individuality, within reason, of course.

At Glacier Interactive Marketing, the office space was wide open with many rafters, and dark, shelved dividers had been installed throughout the area. The design of the office made it challenging to personalize any of the spaces. One of the staff members wanted to do a living wall with plants — her rationale was that if she was going to work in this type of space, she wanted to make it 'her'. The company considered it, but a living wall wasn't feasible. Instead, she then went to secondhand shops and bought interesting objects for the shelves, along with plants, which she paid for personally. Management insisted on reimbursing her because she brought an elegance to the space at such an inexpensive price. A word of caution — if people are allowed to have plants, they need to be responsible for taking care of them. There's nothing worse than an office (or any space) filled with dead plants.

A current question in the workforce — do you allow dogs in your workplace? If the building allows, we're all for it. They give a different feel to the office or any space. And dogs unquestionably are therapeutic. Any of us could be having the worst day (or week) we think we've ever had, but if we have the opportunity to pet a dog for a few minutes, watch it sleeping peacefully, or playing with a toy, it's pretty hard to remain feeling down or angry. The challenge is creating guidelines around the whole scenario. A badly behaved dog is going to cause more harm than good. And badly behaved needs to be defined in some way — just like parents, no one wants to admit that their furry friend is 'a terror'. A dog needs to be friendly, not overly noisy (i.e, barking), and house-trained. It's also critical to ensure prior to going ahead that no one in the office suffers from allergies. If that's the case, there's no point in moving ahead with this initiative. When it works, we can't think of anything else that brings such a nice feeling to an office.

One of our clients has a large dog that is always lying in his bed by the front door of the office. It gets up to come and greet everyone that walks through the door. Even if you're an angry customer when you arrive, it's pretty hard to stay that way. This is a free way to completely change the ambiance in the office. One company we experienced adopted a dog in the name of the company for this very purpose. They created a schedule and people took turns taking care of the dog at night and on weekends. Of course, everyone had to be on board for this, and it was a success. The dog became everyone's dog, the company mascot and it created a significant bond among everyone there. If taking on a dog at the office is too much bother, consider fish, which can be meditative.

During the massive flood in Calgary in June 2013, people still came into work at Big Sky Architecture, although there was no heat and no power. Travis, the COO, made hot chocolate and did coffee runs several times a day. Even when there wasn't an issue with working conditions, he would occasionally call a local food truck to arrive at the back alley and tell everyone to go out and grab lunch on him (or not— the novelty of the food truck being there was perk enough sometimes). It was a 10 minute break out of everyone's day and it was invaluable. These little touches can make all the difference and help people to feel appreciated, which is critical for their experience at work, and for your bottom line.

Many people now walk or bike to work. This is a great idea, but it's challenging for people who bike to work to then have to sponge-bath in the washroom, with others coming into to use the facilities and seeing much more of their colleagues than they want to. A place to change privately is a great benefit; if you can add lockers and showers, it's brilliant. Many people like biking to work, and they end up being somewhat sweaty all day. Having secure bike storage is also becoming important. Putting in a shower is obviously a cost, but your people will be healthier and more efficient if they can exercise every day. Running at lunch time provides wonders for productivity, but most people won't run, walk or bike if there's no shower available. In our experience, the younger generations would rather work in a place that offers those kinds of perks instead of earning another few thousand dollars per year.

If we go back to those small details again, offering a range of beverages, a decent coffee machine, a fridge for lunches and drinks and a microwave, all add up, even on a subconscious level, for the people who work for you every day. Have a fruit bowl so healthy snacks are available, rather than bags of chips or chocolate bars. Create a schedule for people to take turns bringing a weekly box of fruit or hire a fruit delivery service if you can. Another important detail is to ensure you have nice washrooms that are consistently supplied with mouthwash, hand cream and hairspray — these kinds of gestures are so inexpensive but provide huge returns as far as creating the type of workspace your people enjoy coming to everyday.

Some companies bring entertainment into the office such as pool tables or video game consoles/games. That can be successful, or cause its own problems. One of our clients brought in a foosball table but it was so loud, no one could work if anyone was playing on it. So, it just sat there — it was like the exercise bike many have bought for their homes with all the best of intentions, only for it to turn into a handy place to hang clothes. If you see people taking 15 minutes out of the day to take advantage of a quick game in a friendly competition with a co-worker, don't walk by and frown — perhaps stand by and cheer them on. Some of the best ideas come when formality is out of the picture. It needs to be carefully considered and align with your workplace and culture.

The best and most successful companies have engaged, productive and loyal people, most of whom are not there only for the money. Creating and designing a workplace they want to come to every day, a space where they feel 'at home', physically comfortable, valued and appreciated, is one of the best ways to build an engaged workforce who will stick with you, through both the good times and the bad.

CHAPTER 7

Are you listening?

"A unique relationship develops among team members who enter into dialogue regularly. They develop a deep trust that cannot help but carry over to discussions. They develop a richer understanding of the uniqueness of each person's point of view."

PETER SENGE

With every organization, there are opportunities to learn and to grow as a leader or manager, through critical conversations held during different touch-points with your people. One of the most important discussions you can have and learn from is an exit interview, when a person is leaving your company. They are leaving — whatever the reason is, it's important to find out why and what the experience was like for them while working for you. You can discover, through their eyes, what was great and what the problems were during their time there. What do they think needs to be addressed; how do they rate organizational communication and leadership skills within your company? This is the perfect time to get a sense of what it 'feels' like, what the experience has been for the people who work for your company. With every person that leaves your organization, it's critical to undertake this process and to do it thoroughly. The person leaving may represent a gold mine of information for you — they are leaving — they don't have to 'hold back' or remain quiet about concerns or issues they faced.

But, why wait until people are leaving the organization? What if instead, you captured this information while they are still there, hopefully preventing them from leaving at all? We suggest a process we call 'stay interviews'. This is comparable to an exit interview but captures similar information from your people while they are still employed by your organization. Another term for this is a cultural assessment. It's ideal to undertake these interviews on a regular basis (annually, if possible). This way you can see how you have improved year-over-year with the issues that are discovered from this process. If for some reason your results aren't as favourable one year, look into the reasons and come up with a strategy for improvement. Many of the same types of questions will be used as in an exit interview.

These interviews are best done face-to-face. It allows you to read body language and probe further when you think the individual may be holding something back. This is easier and less costly in smaller companies. In larger companies, we sometimes have to resort to an online platform. In this case, we often won't receive as much raw information because we are not sitting across from them in person asking the questions. With an online platform, we also are not able to assess body language or dig deeper when we spot a concern. Some companies choose to hire an outside HR consultant for this purpose, so they can ask the tough questions that are more challenging for people to answer if they are across a desk from someone who has the ability to impact their employment. If you choose to use someone in-house, ensure it is not the person's direct manager. You're unlikely to get honest feedback. Throughout this whole process, it is imperative to promise 100 percent anonymity in the responses. We only provide feedback summaries, not actual quotes or answers that could give the source individual's identity away. With our training and many years of experience we've learned to observe, understand body language and to realize when we're not getting the full answer, so it's apparent to us when we need to keep delving further with more probing questions. If you don't get the truth and full story from individuals in this process, valuable time and dollars are wasted.

Be direct, which will be more comfortable for the interviewee, if the interviewer is an external person such as a consultant. The people working for you typically feel a consultant can be trusted more to keep the responses confidential than another company employee. Another reason for hiring an outside resource is that there is no bias; they typically don't know the stories behind the individuals. They don't try to skew results one way or another. They are hired by the company as consultants, but are not internal human resources staff, who consciously or subconsciously, have a loyalty to the company leaders. It's challenging for them to be neutral. As consultants, they offer that neutrality.

Some organizations carry out these assessments annually in order to create a benchmark from which to build an HR strategy or to fine-tune their existing one. For leadership who want to develop a 6-18 month strategy or improve on the existing one, these assessments are ideal as a starting point. Part of our mandate is to create an environment where they can trust us and be open; we work with them in a way that ensures they will believe in the process. We had one situation where an individual was so skeptical of the process, he didn't want to say anything. We suggested he talk about the weather or sports so that from an optics perspective it looked like he participated in the process. Since these interviews are voluntary, he wanted it to look as if he participated. Once he was given the freedom not to participate, he started talking and this particular interview went on for almost two hours. The information we gathered was invaluable. It's also critical to 'scrub the data' and ensure complete anonymity for everyone. Direct quotes must not be included in any feedback to leaders so that the identity of the person is kept confidential. When you have all the information you need from the original notes and surveys, they should be shredded.

This exercise will make apparent the key themes of how the culture is operating. It is unlikely only one person is experiencing a particular issue. We can find out what's working and what's not, have discussions about how to make it better and address one or two key issues at a time. We also can look at how to promote the things that people love about the company — enhancing the already existing culture.

Once these assessments or interviews have been completed, company owners or leadership need to be debriefed. Our process is to give detailed findings to leadership and higher-level summaries to the people who are employed there. Leaders must be brave at this point — they must be willing to hear the results, and not just hear them, but listen and take action. Most of their people just want to be heard and understood. How we conduct this type of research for clients is carefully considered and planned. We have come across leaders who ask us to tell them which people are giving negative feedback. That's a line we won't cross. People's jobs are on the line and we're cognizant of that.

This is not an easy or inexpensive exercise, but from a human resources' perspective, it's money well spent. From the viewpoint of those working within the company, if it's done the right away, the benefits are priceless — knowing leadership is taking the time to hear what they have to say about the organization and care enough to take action is brilliant. One word of caution, don't overpromise on the results. No matter what the outcome, a company cannot necessarily change everything, especially in the short-term. It is imperative that in the communication, people know that while their input is invaluable, you must look at themes and put together a realistic plan to address over a period of time (typically 12-18 months).

When it comes to feedback or 'disciplinary' conversations, confidentiality is crucial. These conversations need to be one-on-one. We also believe they should be carried out more frequently than most companies currently undertake them. The annual review, for many, is becoming extinct and for good reason. In our view, it's a pointless exercise. If one of your people has made a mistake or missed an opportunity for learning, waiting eight or nine months to address it is a waste of time. You've missed the better part of a year for that person to have benefited from the immediate conversation and to learn and grow from it. Having a discussion at an annual review is no longer meaningful when that much time has passed. It's now history. Also, research shows that millennials want instant feedback; annual discussions aren't valuable with them.

---------------------- ◎ ----------------------

I always advocate having these conversations with your people — there's always room for improvement with everyone. The feedback needs to be factual, transparent and offer solutions for improvement, not just criticism. If someone isn't open to receiving feedback and to pursuing growth, perhaps they're not someone you want in your organization. I've learned over the years to give bad news in a good way. Look at the other person in the face, stick to the facts, don't make it personal and don't sugarcoat it. And then move on, don't dwell on it.

If you don't get it out on the table, you'll stay annoyed and it will affect your relationship with that person and your ability to have a working relationship with them.

—*Wendy*

———————————————— ◎ ————————————————

The key to any discussion, if something needs changing, is to be specific about it. It's not helpful to say something like "you don't get along with your co-workers" — be detailed in what's been observed, what the issue is, and present a solution and a timeline to talk again. Give examples of what you've observed or what's been reported to you, and then provide concrete ways to make the situation better. Don't put yourself in a potential litigious situation but at the core of it all and back to our overall philosophy, the person deserves to hear the truth and be given the chance to change or improve. It's a two-way street. People need to be able to tell their story of what happened, their perception of what occurred. They must be able to tell you if there has been something they need which has been lacking, to ask questions and to be given a voice.

If you're going to do an ad hoc evaluation or a review, do it for the right reasons. At Stampede Manufacturing, Sarah, the President and CEO, wanted to terminate the VP Operations. To achieve this, she made the decision to have Wendy Ellen Inc. carry out what's called a 360 review. If you've never come across one before, a 360 review is a professional feedback opportunity for a group of peers, leaders and clients. What you are trying to accomplish with this type of review is to tap into everyone, inside and outside the organization, who touches that person. The goal is to provide feedback and suggestions for improvement and skills which could be honed. This type of review differs from an employee appraisal which traditionally provides the person with the opinion of his or her performance as viewed by their manager. Because of her bias or agenda, Sarah believed the VP Operations would receive terrible reviews, that he would be 'trashed'. Be careful what you wish for! He received great reviews; he was well liked and respected by everyone. A 360 review is designed to be a positive experience and help someone grow as a leader or manager, not a tool to humiliate them. This exercise backfired completely on Sarah. The VP Operations knew exactly what her motivation was and that she had no intention of using this information as it was intended. Although Sarah tried to keep it to herself, it was clear she was livid. The VP challenged her on the motivation for the review (he often challenged her, and that was one of the things she didn't like). Sarah wanted those who reported to her to be subservient. She also didn't want to hear the concerns of others about her own behaviour. As a leader, she was more like a tyrant or dictator.

These processes need to be undertaken for the right reasons (not for personal vendettas), to get a better picture of how that person is functioning within an organization and externally, if applicable. This type of review is expensive and time-consuming, which is why it's usually only conducted for more senior personnel, so ensure it's done for the right reasons and don't waste it. These also work well for not-for-profit organizations. It can be challenging for a Board of Directors to assess the performance of an Executive Director as they don't work with them on a day-to-day basis. Using a 360 review allows the Board to assess skills from the eyes of all who work with that person.

I recall a situation where I had to give someone terrible 360 review feedback. Kudos to her; she really listened and took the information to heart. She turned her negative 360 review into the most positive thing she had done for her career — she listened and learned resulting in her leadership skills improving tenfold. These reviews have been done annually with the results improving year after year. She now has long tenure with this organization and has a dedicated and loyal staff. You need to be brave to hear negative feedback and not take it personally.

–Ashley

We don't sugarcoat or underplay what we have heard. There are several great tools to use for the betterment of your organization and people, but if they are not used for the right purpose, don't do it. Some companies will undertake these processes — stay interviews, 360 reviews — just to be able to say "We do HR. We have an HR strategy." That's not the point.

When a discussion has to happen, make it a scheduled sit-down conversation and not a 'by the way'. Be careful to plan the timing and the location. Don't do it on the fly — treat the other person with respect and allot a time for the discussion. It's unreasonable to surprise someone with negative feedback as they're standing beside you at the coffee machine or in the elevator. And even more importantly, make sure you have all the facts before speaking to them. Don't begin this type of conversation based on assumptions.

Another aspect that leaders often struggle with when it comes to their people is mental health issues. When it comes to mental health in the workplace, employers have an ethical responsibility if they suspect someone is struggling with this type of health issue. There's a fine line between opening the door to allow an individual to have a conversation with you and breaching their privacy. That's why we stress having an open and friendly culture where everyone feels valued and respected. If your behaviour is similar to that of a top down, tyrant-like leader (otherwise known as a dictator), you can't then do an about-face and suggest to someone they come and talk to you if they feel it's necessary.

While we're certainly not suggesting accusing people of mental health issues, asking someone you're concerned about, how they're doing, how they've been lately or mentioning that they don't seem themselves, is appropriate and necessary. Asking them if they'd like to grab a coffee or chat with HR opens the door to a conversation that allows someone to seek help if they need it. There is no strict legislation around this right now— but one-third of our time is spent at work. As a leader, you have a responsibility to be aware of your people's well-being and open the door to a conversation in the hopes that they will step through and then you can assist them in seeking help. Along with that role, there must be some emotional intelligence where you should be aware if someone is acting differently. That kind of space and opportunity for trust needs to be created and nurtured. It can't be forced and you can't suddenly conjure it up.

Harassment complaints are also a challenge for leadership to manage properly. When a formal complaint is lodged against someone in an organization for harassment of any kind, legislation states an investigation must be conducted. We always recommend engaging a third party because there is a process and protocol which needs to be followed. Investigations are delicate and must be managed with care. The person whom the complaint has been made about needs to know what the complaint is, and the investigation as a whole must be kept confidential. This is, of course, challenging, especially when there are witnesses. As well, a 'he said, she said' scenario can prove to be onerous to get to the truth and in many cases, impossible. As soon as there are witnesses or observers to what happened, it becomes much simpler to substantiate. Frequently, either the complainant or the alleged offender ends up leaving, no matter what the results. The job of the investigator is to determine whether or not the complaint can be substantiated. As investigators and HR consultants, we do provide recommendations, but we are not in a position to dictate what needs to be done after the investigation. Once again, back to our philosophy, both the complainant and the respondent are people. We need to keep that in mind, remove any bias and no matter the outcome, treat each of them with dignity and respect, understanding that behaviours are an accumulation of a lot of 'life' behind them.

Ascertaining malicious complaints is also part of an investigator's challenge when searching for the facts. When a complaint is unsubstantiated, when there is no proof of malicious intent, our hands can be tied. Both the complainant and the respondent should be made aware of the final outcome (they don't have the right to know what actions were taken or other details, but they are entitled to know the end result).

We do our best to protect the complainant against future retaliation and there are directives within legislation to ensure this doesn't happen, but it's a difficult situation to police.

In a situation we were involved in, one woman made complaints against a team of co-workers. She had many personal issues, which came to light during the course of the investigation, but two of the men said, "I don't need this" and left as they had other opportunities.

In our consulting work, we have seen examples of all of these processes being done well. Glacier Interactive conducted stay reviews consistently and frequently. At Big Sky Architecture, Travis, one of the leaders, had the ability to execute excellent critical conversations. He was very astute and intuitive; he knew when something needed to be explored further and if someone was struggling.

"Have you talked to them?"

We can't count how many times we have asked this question. A client will call us and tell us they have a situation. "Have you tried talking to them?" is the first question we ask. The most common response is, "No". And if they haven't, we suggest they do before spending their time and money on our services. Many situations can be resolved by simply talking to your people and not being afraid of saying the wrong thing. Talk from the heart, show empathy and listen! Remind yourself that this is a person sitting across from you and they deserve the same attention and respect as other colleagues or your leader. You may not know the answer or have a solution to the situation afterwards, but you are now aware of what is going on with the person or have a better idea.

A common situation we get asked about is what to do when someone is late all the time or often doesn't show up on Mondays. It's essential to ask them what the problem is that's causing them to consistently miss Mondays (have the data available when you have the conversation). Perhaps they are a weekend warrior and they burn up all their energy on the weekend. A solution could be to go to a four-day week, or start later on Mondays, or change their weekend behaviour. If someone's behaviour is bothering you — it could be the smell of their daily tuna sandwich, or the volume at which they speak on the phone, talk to them before you take the step of going to HR. As human beings, we often make things so complicated. A short, tactful and to the point conversation can sometimes clear up a nagging workplace problem in a few minutes.

When women began working out in the field, my first contract in the HR department of a large company involved managing a situation where one woman was the first and only female to work on their site. One of her male co-workers made a comment that she looked better in coveralls than the rest of the crew. She was upset and offended, and filed a complaint.

The legislation behind these types of things was not sophisticated yet, so I brought them together to discuss what happened. It was quickly resolved — she said she was sensitive about those comments as she was the only woman there, and he thought he was being 'nice' by complimenting her. He immediately realized his mistake. They were friends from that point on.

—Wendy

――――――――――――― ◎ ―――――――――――――

Conversations, remembering that everyone is an individual who has a history and, unfortunately some baggage, is just common sense. In our minds, using practical, sound judgement is the key to a successful resolution to most situations. And it will also help you to avoid litigation. Much of what ends up being a problem, escalating or even making it to the courts and in front of judges, could be avoided, if we all took a step back and took a dose of common sense.

CHAPTER 8

Awkward conversations everyone avoids

◎

It became apparent to me over time that the best way to manage tough conversations is to be direct, to not sugarcoat the problem. I've also learned the discussion becomes less difficult if I start it out by saying "This is going to be an awkward (or a tough, or a challenging) conversation. There's no easy way to say this." And then I state the issue in as clear and simple terms as possible. I try to be as matter of fact as I can be. This clearly opens the door for anything needed to be said. And I also try to inject humour into what I say if it's suitable for the situation. This can be a fine line because you need to ensure the person hearing the message understands the seriousness of the issue, or the point of the conversation is lost.

—Wendy

◎

Over the years we've been consulting, we've run into many awkward, funny and challenging situations where we've been called into help. None of these have been easy conversations; for the majority, we've been asked to 'handle' the matter because no one else wants to be the one to have that conversation. And quite frankly, as HR, that's our role.

One of the most challenging issues we had to deal with was around language. One of our clients had a staff mainly consisting of people of Chinese descent. There was only one English-speaking individual. The issue was that the Chinese staff spoke Mandarin when talking to each other. The English-speaking person increasingly felt isolated, and at times, wondered if they were talking about her. Whenever they were laughing, she felt left out and worried she was being ridiculed. It was one of those workplace conversations that had the possibility of going badly if it wasn't handled with care. The Chinese staff obviously had the right to speak their language and so careful managing of the situation was critical. Our approach when speaking to them was to try to get them to understand how she felt. How would they feel if they were in that situation, in that other person's shoes? In this case, the issue resolved itself for a while, but the majority kept reverting to their own language. It was easier for them, and it was more of an unconscious thing, but they did try to speak English initially. It wasn't their first language and they were clearly much more comfortable speaking Mandarin. The reality in any situation is that there are some problems that can't be completely eradicated. The positive that came out of this conversation is that they became more aware of including their colleague in their conversations where possible.

It can be somewhat of a minefield when approaching some situations. Another challenging one occurred when we were asked to deal with a food issue. In this case, strong smelling soup was brought for lunch by someone every day, cooked in the microwave, and then eaten at their cubicle. Many people brought food from home and prepared it in the microwave at work so it wasn't an unusual practice at this organization. Unfortunately though, the odour of this particular concoction was overpowering and because it was heated in the group microwave, made it even worse. The other people also complained that their food began smelling like the offending lunch whenever they cooked in it. It permeated the whole floor. Similar to the first issue with language, this person wasn't doing anything 'wrong'; she could bring any type of food she wanted to the office. Again, we had to approach it by painting the picture of how it was affecting other people. We couldn't tell her what type of food she was allowed to bring to the office but suggested to her that she be empathetic about how it affected other people. She was embarrassed, which was not the intent but often the outcome. Fortunately, she was receptive and understanding, and the situation resolved itself quickly.

With workplaces being increasingly multicultural and with people working remotely, often in different countries, HR faces the challenge of managing diversity, maintaining working relationships and settling disputes. Cultural diversity can become a serious roadblock to productive teamwork. When you have a team that has been raised in different cultures, how do you create an environment where they can work effectively together? Language, customs, beliefs and working styles are going to clash. Holding informative lunch 'n learn sessions on diversity or even asking someone to host a noon hour session on something to do with their culture often helps to break down the barriers. One client we worked with held monthly 'Meet and Eats' – where one person would present on something interesting to them. It could be a trip, a hobby or a personal project. Many of the presentations ended up being about a cultural practice because those were the most interesting ones. Adopting a similar practice in the office is a great opportunity for everyone to bond and learn about each other. When you have a relationship with your co-workers, things like language barriers or different foods or customs become less of a problem. It is human nature to be less bothered by your friends than strangers!

Religious holidays should be addressed to accommodate different cultures as well. It's important to honour those holidays within the commitments of business. Once again, talk to your people to find out what is important to them and do your best to accommodate; that doesn't mean special privileges, but it may mean swapping Canadian-sanctioned time off with other days off.

The all-time, most awkward conversation I've ever had to have was with an older man who was spitting in the sink in the lunchroom. I realized this may have been a cultural difference, and he had no idea it was offensive to others in the office. It was such an uncomfortable concern to raise with him, the only thing I could do was to say, "There's no way to soften this message, I just don't know what else to say to you, but other people working here have asked that you stop spitting in the sink. Please use the washroom." Not only was this the most bizarre conversation but fortunately, it was also the shortest!

–Wendy

Dress code problems are often an issue, and interesting enough, it's rarely men who violate these rules. What we come across most frequently is women wearing inappropriate clothing — tank tops, too short skirts or dresses, or flip flops. At one of our client's offices, a woman wore pyjamas to work one day!

At another client's, a female staff member would wear sandals to work and then take them off to walk barefoot the rest of the day. This was a law firm and this behaviour raised a lot of eyebrows, even though the firm had a relaxed dress code. It was not only a safety hazard because of what she could potentially step on in the office, but also very unprofessional and unhygienic. When we spoke to her about it, she was defensive and although she then adhered to the code, she was indignant about it. Often when we see this type of response, it can be a red flag and a signal of future problems. This young woman didn't last much longer there. Most individuals who are people you want to hire and retain are self-aware enough to look around and assess what everyone else in the workplace does when it comes to cultural behaviours such as appropriate office wear, lunch time habits and even smoking breaks (which is an entirely different problem in many workplaces). Of course, they can get it wrong, but anyone worth retaining is typically going to be apologetic and quick to remedy their behaviour.

One situation we encountered with a female staff member who was a single mother, and a fairly low income earner, was a problem that needed delicate handling. She honestly thought she was dressed in an appropriate and fashionable way and wore leggings with high boots and a cropped shirt. Leggings can be a great look but the body needs to be covered to an appropriate length. This had to be handled with kid gloves and we were aware she didn't have much disposable income for office attire. Having worked with her for some time, we knew she wasn't aware of her misstep. This young woman was excellent in her role and didn't have many opportunities. We advised our client to bring in a style consultant to the office to speak to everyone about what was appropriate office wear and what was not. We orchestrated a lunch session with the consultant and the client was generous enough to give everyone a gift certificate to a clothing store. This was an excellent solution because it didn't single out this one individual who was really trying to improve her clothing and look the role.

The funniest situation I've ever had to deal with, although it was also way up there as far as the 'awkward' factor, was with a fellow who rode his bike to work everyday. There was no shower at work, so he would remove his biking clothing and stand in the men's washroom completely naked and wash up. Any other men walking in would immediately be faced first thing in the morning with this fully nude co-worker rinsing himself off in the bathroom. Anyone walking by, including women, could see him if someone opened the door and they were at a certain angle. I had to sit him down and tell him, he just couldn't do this anymore. It wasn't appropriate. We were sorry there weren't showers but he had to be far more discreet. What was truly funny is that he saw absolutely nothing wrong with his behaviour.

–Ashley

Another critical and uncomfortable situation at a client's arose when a person on sick leave brought in fake sick notes. We have seen enough legitimate doctors' notes to spot an illegitimate one. Because we were dealing with someone on sick leave (disability being a protected ground for discrimination), any time you deal with an issue like this you walk a fine line. This note was an obvious fake with everything from lack of letterhead to wrong dates to the way it was written. We had to call the individual and clearly ask him to obtain a note from his doctor on the clinic's letterhead with specific dates of illness and possible return to work dates. That person, unfortunately, never returned.

Whenever the conversation is about money, transparency is so critical. You need to set the stage and give an explanation. Because it's about money, you must also be forthright, and not waver. There are a lot of legislative requirements that must be followed when adjusting salary downwards, so a word of caution to ensure you are on top of those requirements, that your people are aware of their rights and you are aware of yours as the employer.

In my own consulting practice, I have had to have difficult conversations with my consultants. Like most business owners, I have a model of doing business I want my people to emulate. Over the years I think I'm doing a good job at picking the right people to espouse our values and service but at times, I can also misjudge. When I receive poor feedback from clients on one of my consultant's performance, it is difficult for me to have those conversations with that person. I am good at coaching others about what to do but when it is in my own shop, it becomes harder. So, I stick to the same advice I give my clients – be honest and upfront. I lay the issue out on the table without anger or blame. We then talk about what we can do to fix the problem. I have to say this works almost 100 percent of the time, when it hasn't, it usually results in a parting of the ways. If someone isn't open to working towards a solution, that may end up being the only answer.

–Wendy

Personal space in an open area office can also cause many issues. Overbearing fragrance, clutter and noise are often the biggest culprits. One person was so sensitive to the smell of perfumes and lotions, he had trouble doing his work. This one was easy — we purchased a high-end air filter to modify his environment and moved him to a corner cubicle. Instead of infringing on the rights of others working there, we modified his work space. This did result in a few other individuals asking for an air filter, but in the long run, it was a minor expense to make the environment more pleasant for all.

As HR consultants, we often come across workplace addiction issues. At one of our clients, an individual phoned in one Monday and advised he wasn't able to come to work; he had relapsed during the weekend. It was the first time there had been any indication of a problem. Addiction is a protected disability, so as an employer, you can't terminate anyone while they are on disability. If a person comes forward and tells you they have an addiction issue, as an ethical employer, you are bound to help them. If you notice concerns, and you currently don't have a documented disability, as an employer, try and assist the person before it does become documented. Not only is it the right thing to do but once there is a bona fide documented disability, there is a great deal of legislation to which you must adhere. One of the best ways to accommodate a person is through your company Employee and Family Assistance Program (EFAP)— every organization should have one. They have the expertise to assess addiction, suggest programs and help with immediate needs of both the employer and the individual. If you don't have an EFAP, hopefully your benefit program covers counselling. In either case, you should allow for the individual to know it is safe to be honest with you as the employer and that you will give them the time and resources to get help. It is important in a situation like this to be firm in your stance that you are giving them a chance to heal, and if they don't take you up on it or don't follow through, you will have to end their employment. There is a fine line between being compassionate and also looking after your business — an employer has to understand where that line is, and it is up to you to ensure your people do as well.

———————————— ◎ ————————————

Wendy is the master of critical conversations. It is a quality I've tried to emulate since day one. It is somewhat of an innate ability but practice does make it a lot easier. To this day, I still remember my first 'awkward conversation' — telling a man that he needed to stop parking in other people's parking spots and pay for his own parking. I was so nervous but the key really was to just be open and concise, and not dance around the situation. I remember thinking afterwards, I couldn't believe I was so nervous about a 30 second conversation that was resolved immediately. Conversations are always worth it!

–Ashley

———————————— ◎ ————————————

Depending on the 'offence', when, after speaking with the person, the behaviour persists, it then has to move towards a disciplinary process. The conversation can happen once or twice to address the issue, but if nothing changes, you need to move to the next step. And, they need to know this will be the next step. As an example, with dress code, if they persist in wearing inappropriate clothing, the next discussion is to tell them if it happens again, they will need to go home and change, and the time it takes to do this will be without pay. When someone won't alter what they are doing, it's time to let them go. In most cases we wouldn't recommend letting them go with cause; it is far simpler to let them go with notice as per employment standards. Again, it's a signal there are bigger issues which you are going to have to face down the road at some point.

As an employer, you are able to terminate employment with anyone at any time — as long as you pay them what they are entitled to in lieu of notice. It's not a pleasant step to take, but when it's a serious issue and is affecting the entire office or team, it's not sensible to keep the person working for you. Their behaviour affects everyone — do the right thing.

We believe in being forthright and calling a spade a spade. If you have to have an uncomfortable conversation, dive in; don't beat around the bush. It can be a cultural difference, or simple ignorance, and they just need to be made aware of it. But remember, especially when it's cultural differences, to tread carefully as the last thing you want to do is offend or insult anyone. Look at each situation separately; remember the person sitting across from you is another human being and often isn't aware their behaviour is causing problems.

CHAPTER 9

I'm good with how things are

*"Leadership is not magnetic personality, that can just as well be
a glib tongue. It is not "making friends and influencing people",
that is flattery. Leadership is lifting a person's vision to higher
sights, the raising of a person's performance to a higher standard,
the building of a personality beyond its normal limitations."*

PETER DRUCKER

From the time we are infants, we create routines to feel secure, organized and in control of our lives. It's no surprise then that most of us view change with at least some level of anxiety and fear, especially when it's being imposed upon us, when we aren't the decision-makers behind what is going to be different in our lives. For the people who are working for you, who typically have no ability to affect the change, how do you help them move forward and thrive in their new environment?

For organizations undergoing change, transparent, effective and frequent communication is critical to helping your people understand and process the news. Not everyone in your company will hear and accept the information in the same way. If the change is a significant one — the sale of the company, new leadership, a reorganization or a merger — create opportunities for them to reach out to ask questions. For some, even an office move is anxiety-provoking. It can be as simple as setting up a special email address for them to send questions, or for others, the ability to have a one-on-one conversation to have their questions answered. Much of how people will react depends on what's changing in their worlds. When the company is adopting new technology or acquiring another business, some are full of anticipation and looking forward to it. Those who are glass-half-full types are naturally going to look for the positive in any situation. If they are the glass-half-empty kind of person, they may need more from leadership or management. Some change events are hard to swing into a positive, such as when a business is looking at downsizing. That's a difficult situation in which to create any positivity. It's always about managing the communication, being honest and transparent about what is occurring and having resources available such as HR or an EFAP (Employee and Family Assistance Program).

In a downsizing circumstance, professional counselling may be necessary for some of your people to manage the situation and be able to function at work during and after the transition. Many people view HR as being equipped to manage every personal issue, but we are not psychologists, therapists or counsellors. As an in-house HR person or as an HR consultant, we can listen and be that ear for people, but we need to be careful not to step outside our wheelhouse. Our mandate in those situations is to provide someone with support and the information to access the appropriate resources.

If it's challenging to provide consistent and frequent communications and updates because of the geography of the company, sometimes we have to get creative. One of our clients was undergoing an acquisition and they had many work sites in locations across the country where some of their people didn't have computers. In that case, we created a weekly poster so everyone who worked on site could be kept up-to-date with what was occurring. Every week, we sent out a new poster to the site managers to hang up where they were visible to everyone. We also ensured there were frequent email communications to those who did have computer access, a Q&A email and a phone number for questions. Not once did we have anyone say to us that it was too much; please don't keep sending us this much information. We don't think you can over-communicate. We have never had the experience where our clients or we were burdening people with too much communication.

One of the other key drivers for accomplishing change in a positive manner is once again for managers and leaders to have a good relationship with their people. They need to know them on an individual basis and understand the level of communication that works best for them. Some will need to process the information on their own; others will need more information and have many questions. It's really important not to take a blanket approach to communicating — we realize that can be difficult in a large organization where there are several hundred or thousand people. If the news can be perceived negatively, such as a reorganization, providing counselling for people is always a good idea. With publicly traded companies, it often happens people don't get the news of an acquisition or merger until the day that it takes effect because of the legalities around the stock indices. Those are hard situations and ones where having the ability to connect with a counsellor is beneficial for the people who are impacted, and for those who remain behind. With mergers and acquisitions, we've seen people called into a boardroom where they watch a video which explains to them that they are no longer with this company; they are now with this one. That's hard for anyone to hear. If you take the time afterwards to explain the reasons — legalities, stock price, jeopardizing the company and so on — once people have time to process the news, they are usually understanding. It's having a bona fide explanation that is critical to them accepting the change.

"The art of life is a constant readjustment
to our surroundings."
KAKUZO OKAKURA

Reorganizations can be hard, whether there are terminations involved or not. In most cases, if possible, advise your people ahead of time that this will be happening. Allowing them to be part of the change process is also helpful; when you ask for input from your team, it helps them to feel like they have some control in the situation. This is not feasible in all situations but when looking at department tasks, structure and efficiency, it's helpful to have input from those on the front lines. It's much better for them to participate, than to just be told after the fact this is how it will be. That's when you will find the most resistance and resentment. We also recommend, in some instances, putting together a steering committee of influential people across the company who have developed strong relationships and connections within the organization to garner information and be the cheerleaders for change.

For teams that have developed a strong bond, bringing on a new leader or a new team member, has the potential to cause waves. Ensure you take the time to onboard the new person properly. An important part of that is to socialize them to the culture. Assuming you have brought in the right person who fits culturally, by doing this well, it can be made seamless for the rest of the team.

When there is a situation where you have to let one or two team members go, it's best again to talk with their co-workers once the deed is done. You don't need to, and quite frankly shouldn't talk about the reasons for the terminations, but do explain to them how the team will move forward and be there to hear their concerns. Again, the more information you can provide about how the work will be carried on in the future and how the person who was terminated is being assisted as best as possible, the easier this transition will be. When there is no communication behind terminations, the people left behind are often fearful that they could be next.

When a large-scale termination is expected, on site counselling is definitely helpful. For those who are not terminated, their experience can be that a long-time co-worker (who may have also become a good friend) is there at 7:59 a.m., and then gone at 8 a.m. People need help to get through these changes; for them it's a loss and one that shouldn't be discounted. The dynamic in a workforce changes drastically with these large downsizings and it is important to assist people in moving forward in the new reality. Cultures will change as a result. This is not a one-time event, but rather one that should be kept on top of until you feel the team come together. This may take longer than you expect.

When managers and team leaders are behind a decision for change, they can be the best advocates. Not everyone is going to like a change incident, but if they have developed strong relationships with their teams and they understand the reasons behind the change, it's easier to get their people onboard. When the change is coming from 'Head Office', and managers and leaders are just the messengers, it is very apparent to their teams. Work with them (the managers) first to help them understand and process the situation. From there, help them to communicate effectively. It will be obvious to their people if they aren't supportive of the decision, so they also need to be provided with the right information from leadership. If they understand the rationale behind it, it's easier for them to be the messengers.

If after all is said and done, the communication around the change is managed poorly, be honest. Take ownership of the fact it wasn't undertaken the way it should have been; tell your people the way you communicated was implemented poorly; share how the situation will be remedied. As best as you can, backtrack on the ineffective communications. Talk to them about what was handled poorly and how it will be better in the future. If you aren't genuine and honest, and call a spade what it is, you will lose integrity in the eyes of your people. By admitting you made a mistake and showing vulnerability, you earn respect. We always advocate also asking what they need — from management and from HR. Give them the opportunity to provide suggestions for the future. By doing this, you gain two pieces of information at the same time and you create goodwill. But … you need to do something with the information. If you ask for it, and then drop the ball by not changing your behaviour in the future or by not implementing any of the suggestions, the situation can become far worse. Their input has been ignored and the perception will be one of disrespect. The resulting reaction will be magnified by the fact the communication was originally done poorly and then the situation will worsen because the contribution you requested is not being taken into account. Pleasing everyone and implementing all of their suggestions won't likely be possible. Pick the popular choices and do something with them. If you don't, you will lose even more respect and goodwill.

We think one of the best pieces of advice we give clients is never to sugarcoat any news or messaging. Honesty and authenticity will get you much further, and if your people perceive you have been dishonest or deceived them in anyway, rebuilding those relationships will be difficult, if not impossible. Obviously, you want to be empathetic to the person who is sitting across from you and deliver any negative news respectfully, but ignoring reality or trying to pretty it up, will always backfire and create an even more challenging situation.

One example of this is was with a client who was purchasing an underperforming small division of about 80 people from a sizeable organization — about 10,000 people. We were consulted on how best to approach the people in the division in the first meeting. Even though they were not reaching their goals, they were still paid and received their benefits because the rest of the company was still making money. Our advice was to talk about the positive aspects of the change, but also to be clear about what the change meant for them. In this situation, the people were initially part of an immense bureaucracy so, in the new company, they would have much more autonomy and the red tape they faced daily to accomplish their work would disappear. On the other side of the equation was the fact that they could no longer ride on negative results. Progress needed to be made and as they were now a stand-alone company, they needed to perform and create results. Face-to-face meetings were held to discuss both the positive and negative possibilities of the acquisition. The conversations were honest and all sorts of questions were asked by the leadership team; the acquiring company had the answers to some of the questions and was transparent about it when they didn't have the information. Their leader was upfront and honest about why they were acquiring the divisions, what the expectations would be and most importantly, the support they would receive. Focusing on the positives motivated the leadership team. A few years later, it is now a strong, cohesive and focused company. Of course, there were hiccups, but what was reassuring was the lack of bureaucracy — issues were managed quickly and transparently so they could carry out the business they were tasked with.

There are many books and articles available that delve into the academics around change management. These are worth a read, but in our practice and client group, we don't think it's that complicated. Again, it's taking a step back and considering the other person and how you would feel in the same set of circumstances. And more importantly, how each of your team members, with whom you've built a relationship, would want to be treated. We don't advocate a lengthy list of steps or procedures to take — sound judgement and empathy will most often be what you need, along with well-thought communication (and plenty of it!).

When your business or organization is undergoing change, remember the people on the other side upon whom the change is being imposed. For them to deal with it — they first must hear it, then they need to understand it, and then they have to have to process it. For each of them, that's going to happen in a range of ways.

CHAPTER 10

What goes around, comes around

---◎---

Everyone who leaves can be
an ambassador for your organization.
People always remember how you treated them.

---◎---

We live in a litigious society today and there are many times during the HR life cycle where you and your company may be vulnerable. Employers have never had to tread more carefully than they do now and ensure that they are not crossing any protected ground — especially at the beginning and end of the HR cycle, during recruitment and termination. Canadian legislation currently prohibits recruiters and HR departments from discussing, or questioning a candidate about age, religion, race or marital status, gender, sexuality, family structure; whether they have pardoned offences and more. In the US, employers are required to keep all the resumes of candidates they have interviewed and to keep all notes of each interview, so an unsuccessful applicant cannot return and claim they weren't hired because of race, gender or anything else covered under a protected ground.

We haven't reached that level of concern yet in Canada, but all indications point to the fact that we are heading in that direction. Employment situations in Canada are becoming more litigious, and we are often brought into consult on strategy or to manage a termination to avoid any potential issues.

At the point where you are exiting someone from your company is the time that you may be most vulnerable to litigation. As with the recruitment phase of employment, a termination cannot be based on anything that falls under the classification of a protected ground. One of the most frequent issues that employers face today is accusations of ageism. We often see bigger payouts these days during layoffs to avoid the appearance of age being a factor. Only in rare cases (for example, when fraudulent activity takes place) do we ever suggest letting someone go for cause. Not only does this prevent them from any notice or severance, it means they are not eligible for Employment Insurance payments. Because of the concerns about a lawsuit, we often advise clients not to terminate for cause. Generally, it will not end well, and the person being let go will find a way to retaliate. Unless, over time, you have built up a solid, documented case for dismissal, or the termination is for criminal activity such as fraud or violence, or a substantiated harassment claim, it is just isn't worth the time or expense involved with a lawsuit. Responding to a claim will likely end up costing you more than paying someone out. We advise our clients to pay, at a minimum, employment standards and save themselves the disruption of defending against a lawsuit. (You often need to pay more than the minimum. If you want the individual to sign a legal release, you will need to pay more than the employment standards legislated amount in exchange for that signature on the release.)

With terminations, depending on the situation, you don't need to treat everyone whom you've terminated equally. As we've talked about throughout this book, even at the termination stage, it's still possible to treat people as individuals. If you're aware of some of their personal circumstances — for example, you know the spouse has also just lost their job — as an ethical employer, you can choose to provide slightly higher severance. Or if they have children, to ensure they have time to take care of doctor and dentist visits, you can extend health and dental benefits so they can get in for prescription refills and a last dental hygiene appointment. If you can, go above and beyond what you are required to do. People who are exiting your organization can be ambassadors for your company and sometimes, even if they are good individuals, the situation may require that you still have to let them go. People always remember how you treated them. Taking into consideration their personal circumstances, if it isn't a big cost or burden to your company, will show that you want to do the right thing. In big organizations, most people being terminated are not allowed to go back to their desks — the supervisor will get their bag and/

or other personal items, and they are walked out by HR or security to the exit. If you can, allow people to collect personal belongings themselves. It's not always possible, but it provides some dignity.

If the person you are terminating has been difficult to work with, you don't need to go out of your way to provide additional support. You can adhere to what is legislated and move on.

With terminations, it's critical to always keep it professional and to stay away from any personal comments or discussions about the 'whys' behind the termination. Everyone wants to know the reason, and everyone wants to have the chance to try and save their job, or change your mind. It's important to remind yourself it's a business decision. Our advice is not to ever get into an involved discussion about it, especially at the termination meeting. In what is often an emotionally charged situation, someone may get verbal and angry, another may be so shocked they don't say anything, while another may cry. We are often brought in to manage the terminations alongside the individual's leader. Because we didn't hire the person, we need a company representative there to officially let that person go. Our job is to de-escalate, to make sure the person understands their rights, the company gets their property, and the individual being terminated gets home safely and with dignity. Our role is to complete the business side first and manage the emotional side second. The manager should only be present for a few minutes to give the message, and then leave, and if possible, take the rest of the team out for coffee to give the person being terminated some privacy and respect.

We help the individual understand the severance package, which can be quite comprehensive. It's important that you do not ask the exiting person to sign a release form right at that point — they are in shock and upset and likely, it wouldn't be considered valid. Keep in mind that they are getting a great deal of information at a highly emotional time – they probably aren't retaining much of what they're being told. Our advice to them is to take it home, review it and seek legal advice, if they choose. As HR consultants, our job is to be understanding, but to ensure the individual knows the news is not going to change — the decision is final.

Because they have received upsetting news, we always make sure they have a safe ride home (we suggest pre-ordering a taxi) and walk them out. Asking security to walk them out sets a bad tone. We also provide our phone numbers and let them know if they need to talk, they can call or text us. Many people want to say goodbye to their colleagues. This is never a good idea right after a termination meeting. Having a coffee with their colleagues at a later time is fine, but they do need to leave the building as soon as they've gathered their belongings. You never know how people are going react; often it's not at all what you expected. One of our consultants had to chase someone running through the office as they wouldn't leave. In these potentially violent circumstances, be cautious, be aware of red flags and be prepared. Being prepared for anything is crucial.

There is a fine line where our expertise ends and it becomes necessary to get legal advice, especially where anything criminal is involved, such as embezzlement and harassment, or if you are terminating for cause. With senior level positions or 'mature' people, it's always good to get a legal opinion as well because case law changes frequently.

While terminations are challenging for everyone, they are a necessary part of doing business. We have worked with some companies that, on occasion, let someone go too quickly, and others that tend to hang on to people well beyond what made sense for the business. One organization we worked with went over and above, well beyond what is reasonable and kept people far longer than they should. Some leaders don't want to end a work relationship for many reasons. They like the individual; they know their circumstances may not be ideal at home; their lives would be devastated if they lost their job, new baby, etc. While these circumstances mean you would feel terrible letting someone go, keeping them to avoid feeling bad about the situation can do far more harm than good to the business. Think of the turmoil that this person is potentially causing others who remain working with you; perhaps they have to pick up the slack, deal with a bad attitude, etc.

There are ways to support those you must terminate to help them move on afterwards. This is where their individual circumstances and a leader's humanity may come into play. Remember your responsibility to those working with you and continue to foster your team. Showing you have the courage (and vulnerability) to let someone go demonstrates strong leadership and shows compassion for those still there. There are several options you can offer as an employer. While it's critical to treat people fairly, sustainability for the business is also equally important.

Understanding an exiting individual's circumstances allows you to tailor a termination package to support them the best you can while still within reason from a business perspective. There are many creative ways to help someone who is going to be let go.

Some of the options you can consider are:

- Salary continuance as opposed to a lump sum termination: you can maintain employee benefits this way (although sometimes not a wise decision either).
- Career transition assistance: you can hire a firm to assist that person in finding their next opportunity.
- Extending health and dental benefits: they can take advantage of psychological counselling or not have to worry about ongoing medical and dental expenses while they look for other work

– in this case you need to ensure life and disability benefits are terminated.

- Provide a mentorship opportunity: someone you know in their profession that can assist on a more informal basis.

Another of our clients, a small plumbing company – Foothills Plumbing — had great retention and many people who had been with the company for a long time. There were two partners: Ken, who had bought into the company after running a family-based business for many years. He was a straight shooter; everyone liked him and he was approachable, although we thought sometimes he could be too accommodating. The other partner was Don — who was one of the original owners and even more accommodating than Ken. He viewed the business as a family and was deeply loyal to his people.

One of their long-term people had developed some mental health issues. She had been working for them for the past ten years; and although their business requirements had changed, they were keeping this individual on because they felt loyal to her. In the end, she was overpaid for what she was able to handle and deliver, but because they felt emotionally tied to her, the owners struggled to find a solution. They tried reducing her role (and her compensation as well). She eventually resigned, stating she wanted to spend more time with her family, which they felt terrible about, and they asked if she would consider coming back part-time on a casual hourly basis. She didn't feel she could handle the inconsistency of part-time work and turned them down. The partners wanted to re-hire her and came to us for advice. Because we're not emotionally involved in these situations, we were able to view it from a neutral perspective. Our advice was not to re-hire her because she was a former staff member with long tenure; it put the company at risk for litigation if it didn't work out. We recommended putting her on a project-based contract with defined terms and hours but also making it clear there was no employment relationship as the contract was based on project work and had a definitive end. In this case, we were concerned the team member was going to take advantage of the relationship. It wouldn't have been that difficult for her to do so because of the history between her and the company. The owners of the company and the long-time staff person were both happy with that solution and they still hire her from time to time for project work.

We've worked for organizations where the leadership is far too obliging to their people — lending them money, giving them increases and bonuses based on need, not on merit, and making closed door, side deals with various individuals. In many cases, there is no consistency and no structure to how they manage their people. While we are definitely advocates for less structure, it's a fine line and there needs to be some baseline rules in place.

We've also witnessed the scenario where an individual will attempt to take advantage of a relationship with the business owner, intentionally or not. When companies lend their people money, what happens when that person resigns, or you need to fire them? How do you recover the loan? Often you don't! Our advice is to give them a bonus if you feel you must do something or if you feel you must give them a loan or an advance, have very clear documentation in writing and signed by both parties on how you will recover the money each pay period, or upon termination. Whether it's personal or business, having boundaries and sticking to them makes for healthier relationships.

On the flip side, there are employers who take the opposite approach — thinking of business only, without regard to the individual or their circumstances (and sometimes how legislation works with circumstances). We need to make sure they understand the individual's situation before making decisions. We often see this with disability cases, impulsive terminations or over-compensation problems. Clients will call us because they want to let the person go; they want to terminate them because they now view them as an annoyance. We often get called in to confirm they can do this and put together the paperwork. There is usually more involved in what's transpiring than what we are told. Our role is to look at the situation and ensure they are adhering to legislation. Once we have confirmed that they are compliant, it's still essential to consider the individual situation. Let's make sure the termination is done fairly and properly, and with enough severance to try and keep the client out of litigation.

With employer rating websites and social media, there are many ways people can hurt your reputation as a company and as an employer. Whether a termination was justified or not, if a person leaves disgruntled and feeling like they were treated unfairly or without dignity, all it takes are a few keystrokes and you will have no recourse. Try and do what's right to avoid this from occurring.

As we mentioned earlier in this chapter, people who leave your company can be your ambassadors. If they have resigned for a different opportunity or been terminated because of economic conditions, they can be your greatest advocates. In an ideal world (with some exceptions, of course), why wouldn't you want them to return after getting experience elsewhere and to bring that new knowledge and skills back to your organization? At one point, they were a valuable part of your team. During the time they have been away, they've hopefully gained professional and personal experience. Having them return, with all their previous and new knowledge, could be valuable to your company and your bottom line.

CHAPTER 11

Just common sense
(Our only HR Best Practice)

————————————— ◎ —————————————

Definition of common sense:
sound and prudent judgment based on a simple perception
of the situation or facts
-Merriam Webster-

————————————— ◎ —————————————

Many HR professionals would argue with us that there is, and needs to be, best practice. When it comes to large organizations, we agree they do need to have their own HR best practices. In the space we work in — small to medium-sized — it's a given that we need to be legislatively compliant and ethical. Beyond that, our only HR best practice is to remember you are talking to a person, not just an employee.

Often, it's the obvious that is overlooked — it should be 'people' management, not 'employee' management. As we've written earlier, successful organizations make people, along with the bottom line, the focus. These leaders know their people; what they are like as individuals, how best to work with them to make it a fulfilling experience, and be as accommodating as they can be within reason. Using common sense and empathy when dealing with any individual situation is the right approach. This, in turn, feeds the bottom line. There's always going to be bad apples and exceptions, but that's what they are — exceptions. Most people want to do a good job, want to be treated well and make their leaders look good.

─────────── ◎ ───────────

*We prefer to come from a glass-half-full perspective;
let's take the positive approach and give people the
benefit of the doubt first.
For most people, that works.*

─────────── ◎ ───────────

Why this works so well for our clients is simple. Similar to the education system, where some children don't excel in the regular public school environment, putting your people in a box at the office may create success for some, but it doesn't work for everyone. Although our world is often structured to fit within a square box, consider the circles, look at the circles, triangles, rectangles, etc. — do you need to make them fit within that box structure? If the work is being done and you are achieving the results you're after, does it matter whether or not you can make your people fit into that rigid structure?

It's been our experience over many years, that leadership who understand that concept, have reduced people management issues, higher retention and an engaged workforce. These organizations also have a healthier bottom line as a result. Why? Because leadership is able to focus more on the business and on strategy, and less on putting out fires that arise because an unhealthy culture exists in their organization. When you aren't spending your days trying to solve unfortunate and often unnecessary issues with your people, there's more time to spend focused on revenue creation and working towards your goals.

That type of culture is achieved because of great leadership. Whether it's the CEO, manager or team lead, they view their people as the organization's most important asset; healthy sustainable cultures are created from the top down. Just as some people are natural born leaders, others are not — those skills can be honed, but it is difficult, if not impossible, to go from being someone without leadership skills to becoming a good or great leader. Promoting highly skilled people who don't have those traits is a mistake; there are other solutions to reward them.

At companies where leadership wasn't willing to change, didn't believe in our approach or didn't value Human Resources, we were typically there in name only. Some leaders want to be able to say their organization has an HR presence because they feel they 'should'. In those situations, it's difficult or impossible to effect change. At Stampede Manufacturing, one of the clients we described earlier, we were only engaged there for about two years. Because of Sarah's leadership style and disregard for the work of a human resource professional, we can't honestly say we were able to improve the culture in her organization. She just wasn't interested in her people as individuals.

The cost of treating people poorly is high. Aside from the tangible expenses of rehiring and retraining and not achieving your goals, the intangible costs must be considered. Those include disruption to your team and your organization's reputation (once a bad review is on social media, it's there forever). Great leaders should aim to make their organization a place where people love to come to work.

Consider what it really means to make your people a priority. When you hired that person, you made that decision for a reason. How can you make the experience of every person you work with the best it can be?

To us, this is common sense and that's why we are very good at what we do. It turns out that it's not common sense to everyone — and that's why we wrote this book. As human beings, we often complicate life unnecessarily.

As with everything, it's in the details. It's the simple gestures that can reap big rewards — starting at day one when someone walks through the door to start their new role with your organization. Make sure that first day is a welcoming one, take the time to get to know them on an individual basis quickly, later on stop to say hello and to check-in. Find out what success

at work means for them and help them to achieve it. Address problems —
yours and theirs — with transparency and conversation.

Take a moment to imagine the difference in your workplace. Your
people will be more engaged and more productive because they have been
given the opportunity to aim towards their own individual idea of success.
Because they feel valued, they will be motivated to support you in your
own path. Your people will be inspired by you, a great leader.

——————————————— ◎ ———————————————